Research Report No. 104

Adebayo O. Olukoshi

The Elusive Prince of Denmark

Structural Adjustment and
the Crisis of Governance in Africa

iska Afrikainstitutet
Uppsala 1998

Indexing terms

Structural adjustment
Governance
Democracy
Aid policy
Africa

ISSN 1104-8425
ISBN 91-7106-428-1
© the author and Nordiska Afrikainstitutet 1998
Printed in Sweden by Motala Grafiska, Motala 1998

Contents

Introduction

There has, recently, emerged a growing concern among scholars and policy makers, including bilateral and multilateral donors, to establish and elaborate a connection between structural adjustment and governance in Africa, Latin America, and Asia. This concern has been driven primarily by the desire for more tangible results from the on-going quest for market-driven economic reform in the adjusting countries of the Third World, especially those of Africa. It has resulted in the devoting of increasing intellectual and material resources to the study of the ways in which the framework for political, legal, and administrative governance can be better made to complement the reform objectives represented by the structural adjustment programmes (SAPs) championed by the International Monetary Fund (IMF) and the World Bank.

Although there is not one universally accepted definition of governance, even among the bilateral and multilateral donors who have built it into their policy packages, there is now no doubt that many scholars and Western policy makers see an organic inter-connection between the politico-administrative and legal framework of the adjusting countries of Africa and their prospects for "successful" and "sustainable" market-based economic reform and generalised recovery. This inter-connection has been variously expressed in the literature: for some (Carter Centre, 1989), attempting to reform African economies without addressing issues of governance is like seeking to undertake a programme of *perestroika* without a simultaneous policy of *glasnost*. For others, like the World Bank (1994b), armed with the benefit of hindsight, it is now claimed to be quite clear that a quest for structural adjustment without a governance component would be tantamount to having "... *Hamlet* without the Prince of Denmark".

This study is concerned to assess the implications for governance in Africa of the design and implementation of IMF/World Bank structural adjustment as part of a wider quest for establishing the case for closer attention to be paid to democratic practices and the democratic aspiration of the peoples of Africa in the formulation and operationalisation of efforts at economic reform. It is a key assumption of the study that politics is central to the design and implementation of any economic reform project, particularly one as ambitious and all-embracing as the structural adjustment programmes of the IMF and the World Bank. On the face of things, this assumption will appear to coincide with the increasing concern to factor politics into the imple-mentation of economic reforms associated with the World Bank's recent "political economy" (World Bank, 1994b) and the public choice approach that has grown in popularity since the late 1980s. However, we differ from both the Bank and the public choice theorists insofar as ours is not a concern to "save" the neo-liberal adjustment project by seeking ways, including those that are clearly Machiavellian (Waterbury, 1989, for example), of subordinating politics and political actors to the demands of the orthodox structural adjustment model in the belief that it is a model that is essentially coherent, settled and inevitable, the only challenge left being to (re-) orient politics and public administration in its support.

Underlying our own assumption on the centrality of politics to the process of economic development is the view that the structural ad-justment framework for economic reform should, itself, be open to problematisation and be seen as a legitimate target for contestation and reformulation by the social forces which must bear the costs of its implementation under donor pressure. There is nothing sacrosanct or settled about the neo-liberal structural adjustment model; persistence with it in the framework of popular disaffection may, in fact, com-pound Africa's crisis of governance. We therefore question the under-lying assumption that informs the World Bank's "political economy" and the thinking of the public choice theorists that the problem in Africa today is not so much with an orthodox economic reform model, which is both "rational" and aims to restore "rationality" to African economies, but with the framework for politics and governance which is essentially "irrational" and "dysfunctional" on account of all-pervading "(neo-)patrimonial" structures and processes built into the post-colonial state form.

We take the view that precisely because of problems that inhere in the design, initiation, and implementation of IMF/World Bank struc-tural adjustment, the quest for the Prince of Denmark within its boun-daries will remain elusive. What Africa needs is not so much "good" governance defined in narrow technocratic, functionalist terms that are meant to further the goals of an adjustment model that is as con-troversial as it is contested but a system of *democratic governance* in which political actors have the space to freely and openly debate, negotiate and design an economic reform package that is integral to the construction of a new social contract on the basis of which Africa might be ushered into the 21st century.

Background Context to the Governance Debate

When structural adjustment first made its entry into the economic policy environment of Third World countries, there was very little direct, explicit or formal concern within the World Bank with political (or "political economy") questions generally and issues of governance particularly. This was so in spite of the fact that the neo-liberal adjustment model carried its own specific political-ideological load and the process of securing its adoption by African governments involved explicit political manoeuvring not only in terms of the deployment of a host of conditionality and cross-conditionality clauses, but also through the attempts by officials of the multilateral financial institutions to forge links with state officials who were thought to be most receptive to the aims of the programme.

There were, of course, policy intellectuals (Deepak Lal, 1983 and 1987, for example) who quite early in the implementation of the adjustment programme were very clear about the regime types that they thought were required to ride roughshod over domestic interest group resistance to the implementation of the IMF/World Bank reform package. It was, however, only in 1989, almost a decade after the implementation of structural adjustment began in earnest in Africa, that the Bank first used the term "governance" in its discussion of Africa's developmental problems (World Bank, 1989). It marked the beginning of an open and explicit entanglement by the Bank with politico-legal and administrative issues even if protestations continued from within the institution that its mandate precluded intervention in the internal political affairs of its members (World Bank, 1994a). It is a protestation which always has been and remains essentially formal.

There were two broad and inter-connected developments, one intellectual, the other linked to the end of the Cold War, which provide the context for the open embrace by the World Bank and the rest of the donor community of issues of governance. Regarding the intellectual context, there emerged, in the period from the second half of the 1980s, a growing concern to move beyond the narrow *macro-economic* terms within which the tone for much of the early debate on structural adjustment was set to address broader *macro-political* and *macro-social* issues which, in the view of sympathetic critics of the Bank, operating mostly within the public choice theoretical approach, had been neglected. Growing international concern about the social costs of adjustment implementation, epitomised by the publication in 1987 of UNICEF's plea for "adjustment with a human face" (Cornia *et al.*, 1987), combined with the increasing awareness of the lacklustre performance of the adjustment policies in tackling Africa's deepening economic crisis to propel interest in the analysis of the political and administrative context for economic reform and how they might be managed. This interest fed into the Bank's own quest for credible explanations for the limited achievements of the adjustment model in stemming Africa's economic decline even after the overwhelming majority of the countries on the continent had embraced the reform package .[1]

Initially, Bank officials, responding to criticisms about the failure of the "magical" forces of the market to stem Africa's economic crisis, argued that it was too early to pronounce on the efficacy of policies that were aimed at undoing some 30 years of accumulated distortions. In any case, the African "predicament", bad as it was, would have been even worse had structural adjustment not been introduced, this in spite of the fact that many countries left it very late before taking "painful" but "necessary" steps towards reform. Later, the explanatory framework shifted to the view that the persistence of the African economic crisis had to do mainly with widespread "slippage" and the lack of "commitment" to the reform package by the local policy and political elite. Most African governments were accused of adopting a "stop-go-stop" approach to adjustment implementation which worked to the detriment of a speedy overall economic recovery.

Attempts were also made by the Bank to demonstrate that those countries which showed more "will", "courage", or "commitment" in the course of reform implementation (the so-called "strong" adjusters) generally recorded a better economic performance than those, the so-called "weak" adjusters, which did not show an appreciable level of "commitment". Side by side with this, exercises were carried out aimed at comparing the situation in African countries before and after adjustment implementation with the conclusion pointing, predictably, to the improvements that occurred after the embrace of market-based reforms. Countries with adjustment programmes were also compared with those without adjustment programmes with the conclusion suggesting, again predictably, that the former did better on the whole than the latter. However, these efforts at explaining the impact of adjustment implementation neither failed to dent growing criticism of the adjustment package on account of its adverse social costs nor succeeded in concealing evidence of its limited economic achievements.[2] It was against this background that some scholars began to raise doubts about the efficacy of efforts at adjustment implementation without proper cognisance being taken of issues of "political governance". Thus it was that concern with the "political economy" of structural adjustment began to emerge as an industry in its own right.

The questions which were raised within the framework of this "political economy" were many and varied: Why do governments find it difficult to embrace programmes of economic reform and why do they leave it so late before introducing reform measures? Can economic adjustment occur without a simultaneous programme of political and administrative reforms? What opportunities for coalition politics exist in the promotion of "necessary" economic reforms? Which sections of the state elite can be expected to be reliable allies in the quest for market-led reforms? How might technocrats be "insulated" from undesirable interest group pressures that might compromise the integrity of the adjustment package? What capacities exist locally for initiating or grasping orthodox market reforms? What lessons can be learnt about the timing, phasing, and sequencing of reform policy implementation? Which regime types are best suited for structural adjustment implementation? How might the "winners" from structural adjustment be supported to constitute a local resource for the programme and how might "losers" be compensated, out-manoeuvred, or side-stepped in order to prevent them from obstructing the implementation of the programme? (Lal, 1983, 1987; Callaghy, 1989, 1990; Nelson, 1989, 1990; Waterbury, 1989; Grindle and Thomas, 1991; Haggard and Kaufman, 1989, 1992; Widner, 1992; Bates and Krueger, 1993; Haggard and Webb, 1994).

The question of how "winners" from the reform process could be constituted into a politically viable and durable coalition for market-based economic policies was soon to flower into a full-scale discussion about the necessity for "local ownership" of the adjustment programmes and how this might be bolstered. As we shall see later, this concern with the "political economy" of adjustment, enthusiastically embraced by the Bank in what has been described as an internal "paradigmatic shift" (World Bank, 1994b), dovetailed into the main issues which were being debated within the public choice theoretical approach.[3] The hallmark of this "political economy" is its spirited attempt to transpose some of the key assumptions and categories of neo-classical economics to the arena of politics. That is why, although some of the public choice theorists would opt for a slightly broader perspective on governance than the Bank, this can only be little more than a difference of emphasis within the club, united as they are by a common set of assumptions about the nature of politics.

The growth of interest in the governance issues associated with structural adjustment implementation was strengthened by the international political changes largely triggered off by Mikhail Gorbachev's twin programme of *perestroika* and *glasnost* and the eventual termination of the East-West Cold War as we once knew it (Beckman, 1992; Gibbon, 1992; Mkandawire, 1994). The wave of "democratisation" that swept through the former Soviet bloc, including the defunct Soviet Union itself, towards the end of the 1980s and in the early 1990s and the evident resurgence of consciousness, on a global scale, with regard to questions of "democracy", "human rights", and "popular participation", however defined, fed into and reinforced the intellectual debates that were developing about economic reform and governance in Africa.

So too did the earlier experience of the countries of Latin America with transitions from military to civilian rule through elections served to underline the urgent necessity to address the possible linkages between economic reform and the framework for political and administrative governance in Africa, especially as countries such as Argentina, Brazil, and Chile where political reforms had been undertaken began to enjoy some modest economic growth. Within Africa itself, the end of the Cold War exposed many regimes for the first time to the full force of domestic political pressures for reform from which they were previously shielded by one or the other of the Cold War rivals in their quest for the maximisation of strategic/geo-political advantages. As several authoritarian African regimes and life presidencies buckled under sustained popular domestic pressure for political reforms and many others were compelled to abandon, formally at least, their political monopoly and concede multi-party elections, the interest in the question of governance became even more central.

Although, on the face of things, it would seem that much of the current interest in the subject of economic reform and governance emanates from the international donor agencies active in Africa, especially the World Bank, it is important to emphasise at this stage that long before the donor community turned its attention to this question, numerous African groups and social forces had been involved in struggles for the expansion of the political space on the continent as well as for the creation of structures of governance that would permit the will of the majority of the people to prevail. This is evident from the entire history of the anti-colonial struggle which was as much about political reforms as about economic and social change with a view to enhancing individual liberties and popular participation.

The early post-colonial period, characterised by the abandonment, in many cases, of the African anti-colonialist nationalist project, also witnessed spirited struggles against the imposition of one party and military rule, the institution of personal rule with all of the clientelist networks woven around it, the proliferation of corruption and bureaucratic red-tape, and the spirited efforts at various levels aimed at the de-politicisation of the people. These struggles continued with varying levels of intensity until the mid-1980s onwards when, with the rapidly changing international environment to which we drew attention earlier, the domestic social forces for change in the way Africa had been governed politically and economically were emboldened and re-asserted themselves to unleash popular pressures for political reform towards the end of the 1980s (Anyang' Nyongo, 1987; Mamdani et al., 1988; Mamdani and Wamba-dia-Wamba, 1995).

So strong were the domestic pressures for political and economic reforms in Africa towards the end of the 1980s, and so massive was the level of popular participation in the struggle for change that some commentators (Legum, 1992, for example) were to remark, rather hastily, that Africa was on the threshold of a "second liberation".[4] Whereas the first liberation resulted in the historic defeat of the forces of colonialism, the "second liberation" was leading to the defeat of personal, autocratic rule within the framework of a system of political monopoly either by a single party or by the military. It was expected that this "second liberation" would result in the emergence of an era of "democratic" governments that promote "rational" economic policies. Yet many of those who popularised this view, fascinated as they were by the images of tens of thousands of African men, women and children (hitherto considered as politically docile), actively demanding political reform, hardly bothered to examine the democratic content of the demands and the sustainability of democratic change in the context of deepening economic crises, prolonged structural adjustment and the resurgence of competing ethnicities (Olukoshi, 1995).

Be that as it may, there is no doubt that the confluence of domestic and external pressures for political and economic reform in Africa reinforced the impetus in the scholarly and donor communities to develop a keen interest in the linkage between adjustment and governance on the continent. As we shall see, the World Bank was to immerse itself fully into the governance issue, attempting as it did, to bring its peculiar bureaucratic/technocratic interpretation to bear on the operationalisation of the term. A category of donors, namely

Western governments and their official aid agencies, even went on to embrace a new "political conditionality" under which economic aid was tied to the progress of African governments in introducing political reform and respect for human rights (Mkandawire, 1994; Olukoshi and Wohlgemuth, 1995; Stokke, 1995).

Yet, the notions of political and economic reform which the donors have generally attempted to promote in Africa run counter to those held by the main bearers within the continent of the struggle for democratisation and popular participation. Whereas, to cite one example, the donors see structural adjustment and what some World Bank officials describe as "good governance" as being compatible, many of the social forces in the vanguard of the struggle for democratisation not only reject the structural adjustment programmes but also insist that they are incompatible with popular participation and responsive, democratic governance (Beckman, 1988, 1990, 1992; Bangura and Gibbon, 1992) (see, also, Box 7). At the root of these conflicting positions between the democratic forces pushing for change in Africa and the donors championing reforms are sharply differing perceptions of the African problem. Let us now examine the theoretical sources of these differences as they relate to the governance debate.

Structural Adjustment and Governance
—The Theoretical Context and Contestation

Structural adjustment programmes were introduced into Africa on a massive scale from the early 1980s onward at a time when most African economies were already caught in deep crises of accumulation. These crises manifested themselves not only in terms of rapidly declining output and productivity in the industrial and agricultural sectors but also in terms of worsening payments and budget deficits, acute shortages of inputs and soaring inflation, growing domestic debt and a major problem of external debt management, decaying infrastructure, a massive flight of capital and declining *per capita* real income, among others. The reform programmes which were introduced under donor pressure and implemented under the supervision of the IMF and the World Bank were, ostensibly, aimed at stabilising the African economies, re-structuring the basis for accumulation, and permitting the resumption of growth (Tarp, 1993; Gibbon and Olukoshi, 1996). What the medium- to long-term effects of the adjustment programmes would be not only on the economy but also on society, the practice of politics and the processes of administration became the subject of a major theoretical debate involving two broad schools. The differing positions articulated by both schools, namely, the neo-liberal "political economy"/public choice and the radical political economy schools, are, in many respects, a function of their understanding of the sources of the African economic crises and the role of the post-colonial state in the developmental process.

The Neo-Liberal "Political Economy"/Public Choice School

Championed largely by Africanists based in North American universities and soon embraced by the World Bank as it developed its "political economy" of African development, the neo-liberal "political economy"/public choice school rests on the assumption, whether explicitly stated or not, that "democracy" and economic liberalisation are two sides of the same coin.[5] It takes as its starting point, the view that the post-colonial African state, by its very nature and, therefore, by definition, is at the heart of the economic and governance crises pervading the continent. This state, stripped of the most basic checks and balances of the (late) colonial period, has failed signally in its developmental mission on account of various inter-related factors: its "excessive" and "counterproductive" intervention in domestic economic processes to the detriment of market forces and the private sector; its over-bureaucratisation and bloated size; the domination of its apparatuses by clientelist networks and an "urban coalition" that orients it against the rural (productive) sector and "rational" macroeconomic policies; its submission to "rampant/macro populism" as it panders to a vociferous "urban coalition"; its monopolisation of the main economic levers in society with the resultant proliferation of rent-generating/-seeking niches/activities; and its over-centralisation of development which has discouraged local (private) initiative.

Underpinning the failure of the post-colonial African state, making it an almost inevitable outcome, is its essentially "(neo-) patrimonial" nature and the "rent-generating/-seeking" motivation of African policy makers. These have been central to the adoption by the state of policies that "distort" markets through protectionist tariff and non-tariff barriers, misguided import substitution industrial development programmes, overvalued exchange rates, artificial price-fixing/price controls, a host of subsidies, and the preference for state monopolies. In extending its reach as part of its goal of achieving short-term political order, the state has encouraged the proliferation of patronage institutions and networks which help to consolidate the position of a legitimacy-hungry elite by enabling it, in part, to "buy" the support and/or acquiescence and silence of other social forces while it dips its snout deeply and uninterruptedly into the public trough. Given the domination of the economy by the "(neo-)patrimonial" state or by a "(neo-)patrimonialist" state logic, it is not surprising that the failure of the state easily translates into the failure of the economy. This is made especially so as the fragility of the patronage networks and structures that underpin the state means that they must constantly be re-constituted, producing, in the process, acute regime and/or policy instability and resource misallocation on a stupendous scale to the detriment of long-term national development (Bates, 1981; Sandbrook, 1985, 1986, 1991; Joseph, 1989; World Bank, 1989; Barkan, 1992; Hyden and Bratton, 1992; Landell-Mills, 1992; Widner, 1992).

So central to the discourse of the neo-liberal "political economy"/ public choice theorists was their thesis of the "neo-patrimonial"/" rent-seeking" sources of the failure of the post-colonial state that much of their intellectual output was devoted to producing a host of adjectival appellations that were thought to best capture its nature and *modus operandi*. Thus, in the course of the 1980s and early 1990s, depending on the taste and preferences of particular authors within the school, the post-colonial state was variously characterised as "prebendal", "parasitic", "personalistic", "clientelist", "kleptocratic", "unsteady", "over-extended", "predatory", "crony", "soft", "weak", "lame", "rentier", "sultanist", and, finally, "neo-patrimonial". The appellations served essentially to underline the perceived negative role of the state in the economy and society. In so doing, they reinforced the World Bank's own spirited efforts at stereotyping the state as both inherently ineffective and illegitimate.

The adverse perception of the state and its role in the works of the neo-liberal "political economists"/public choice theorists often contrasted sharply with the approving terms in which they discussed the private/voluntary sectors. This perception also fed into the state-retrenching logic of the IMF/World Bank structural adjustment model, a retrenchment process which, in practice, not only involved the curbing of state expenditure, the retrenchment of many public sector employees, and the privatisation/commercialisation/outright liquidation of public enterprises but also spirited efforts at reforming the civil service (ostensibly to make it "leaner" and "fitter"), curbing the interventionist ambience of the state, and limiting it to the provision of an "enabling" environment for private sector-led development.

In the view of the neo-liberal "political economy"/public choice theorists, structural adjustment which is aimed, *inter alia*, at encouraging the emergence of economic "rationality" through the unfettered rule of the impersonal forces of the market and the promotion of the growth of the private sector should be beneficial for the emergence and sustenance of democracy and a better system of governance than the "neo-patrimonial" structures that pervade the continent and which underlie public policy. Democratisation, signalled by the dispersion of power away from the one-party state and state monopolies, should, in turn, help to break the hold of "minority" urban-based interests on economic policy to the benefit of the rural poor and the army of informals (Herbst, 1990).

Elaborating this position, Larry Diamond argues that part of the reason for the failure of democracy to sink roots in Africa has had to do with the fact that the bourgeois class which could have championed it was either non-existent (because of state domination of the economy) or too heavily dependent on the state and immersed in compradorial, rent-seeking activities. Structural adjustment, in altering the basis for economic activity, will encourage the formation of a bourgeoisie more grounded in production and, therefore, much more autonomous of the state. It is this bourgeoisie that will, out of self-interest, seek to promote democratisation and a more open system of government not based on clientelism, neo-patrimonialism, or prebendalism. For Diamond (1988:27), therefore,

> ... the increasing movement away from statist economic policies is among the most significant boosts to the democratic prospects in Africa.

In addition to the expectation that structural adjustment will "sanitise" African economies and lead to the creation of a non-parasitic bourgeoisie that will then bear the flag of democracy and transparent governance, the "new" "political economy"/public choice theorists have also argued that the process of the retrenchment of the state should result in the strengthening of civil society and associational life which, in turn, should enhance Africa's democratic prospects. The adjustment programme, by emphasising the role of the private sector and encouraging the channelling of resources to private, non-state groups will not only help to "thicken" civil society, that bastion of liberty and democracy, but will also generate interest at the level of society in how the state is governed. Not a few studies have been published within this framework celebrating the rise and activities of voluntary associations and non-governmental groups in civil society (Azarya and Chazan, 1987; Bratton, 1989, 1990; Chazan, 1988; Rothchild and Chazan, 1988).

Attempts have been made by several scholars working within the neo-liberal "political economy"/public choice approach to show that the vacating by the state of certain economic and social spheres as part of the process of structural adjustment has helped to stimulate the rise of voluntary and non-governmental groups and thus promoted the pluralism essential for democracy and transparent governance. Closely related to the flowering of associational life is the growth in informalisation as various individuals and groups, unable, for a variety of reasons, to gain or maintain access to the state and the resources it controls, "disengage" from it and move into the parallel economy and, in so doing, extend the process of informalisation and the "liberterian" and "democratic" impetuses which it (inherently) carries.

Viewed historically, it is difficult not to be astonished by the one-sided anti-statism that underlies much of the neo-liberal "political economy"/public choice approach. The international environment at the time when most African countries attained independence was decidedly in favour of state interventionism in the development process (Killick, 1989; Chaudry, 1993; Mkandawire, 1995; Olukoshi, 1996; Havnevik and van Arkadie, 1996). This, essentially, was as true for the centrally-planned economies of the East bloc as for their capitalist rivals in the West. It was also as true for the developing as for the developed countries. As it pertained to the developing countries, including those of Africa, a variety of theories, ranging from the "big push" approach to the "Gerschenkron thesis", was developed and popularised in support of an interventionist role for the state in the struggle against underdevelopment. From the late 1970s, however, as the neo-liberal ideology gained in ascendancy, the interventionist role of the state in the development process came under severe attack. From being the cornerstone of development, the state now came to be seen as the millstone holding back a system of market-led development.

Yet, the impression created by the neo-liberal "political economy"/public choice school that the role of the post-colonial African state in the development process was wholly "dysfunctional" and that only unremitting stagnation characterised African economies under the regime of state intervention flies in the face of the evidence available on the growth levels which were achieved by African countries in the 1960s and during part of the 1970s (Mkandawire, 1995; Gibbon and Olukoshi, 1996; Havnevik and van Arkadie, 1996). In fact, record growth rates, in some cases as high as 9 per cent, were recorded by many African countries during the period to the early 1970s, growth rates which far overshadow the rare 3–4 per cent average growth rates which have been celebrated as "quite good" during the structural adjustment years of the 1980s and 1990s.

In selectively painting a picture of failure with which to adversely stereotype the post-colonial state, the neo-liberal "political economists" attempt to make the case for their own alternative, largely idealised vision of the role which African states should play. They push for a minimalist state whose role is to produce an "enabling environment" for the functioning of an essentially self-regulating market economy based on free competition—and the "thickening" of civil society. This is a vision of the economy and of the role of the state in it which corresponds to no known actual experience in the recent history of the world (UNRISD, 1995). But it is one which many of the neo-liberal "political economists" felt able to advocate as they sought to transpose the assumptions and categories of neo-classical economics into political science.

Precisely because of the attempt to transpose the categories of neo-classical economics to the political arena and to use these to designate social institutions and actors, the neo-liberal "political economy"/public choice school produces a set of rigid dichotomisations opposing the state to the market, the rural to the urban, the formal to the informal, agriculture to industry, and civil society to the state. Yet, as Bangura and Gibbon point out, this approach to seeking to grasp the African reality overlooks the fact that most of the relations designated by these categories systematically interpenetrate and overlap one another (Bangura and Gibbon, 1992). For, a key characteristic of African economies and societies is the prevalence of "grey" areas which blur and, sometimes, blend the dichotomisations that are central to the arguments of the neo-liberal "political economy"/public choice approach. This suggests that, contrary to the assumptions of the neo-liberal "political economy"/public choice school, a correct reading of the politics of reform in Africa cannot be obtained from deductions deriving from the kinds of rigid dichotomisations that are integral to their analyses. The reductionism that pervades this approach perhaps explains why the World Bank and its sympathetic critics have repeatedly and systematically misjudged and misread the effects of structural adjustment in Africa (Gibbon et al., 1992).

Furthermore, for many of the neo-liberal "political economy"/public choice theorists, civil society and informalisation are treated too uncritically as the arena of democracy and democracy itself is defined in largely functionalist, managerial terms. Additionally, they embrace the structural adjustment model uncritically, accepting at face value the objectives which its authors attribute to it and ignoring the vigorous contestation that has been going on concerning its basic assumptions and the consequences of its implementation. Also problematic is their elevation of "neo-patrimonialism" and "rent-seeking" to the status of an explanatory *deus ex machina* which does not allow for the validity of other motivations for the actions of social actors, including the state. Moreover, their identification of power and exploitation exclusively with the state has been criticised for failing to acknowledge that power relations and exploitation can also be, and are, indeed, found in civil society.

In other words, like the state, civil society also embodies contradictory tendencies and processes which its uncritical equation with democracy conceals. Thus, civil society is not, exclusively, a domain of "liberty" and "democracy" and the tendency to oppose it to the state in a one-sided manner hardly helps to deepen our insights into the ways in which the two inter-penetrate. Finally, there is nothing self-evident that the creation/existence of a private capitalist class "autonomous" of the state will necessarily be supportive of democracy in Africa. Numerous empirically-based studies carried out on the politics of the private capitalist class and its organisations in various African countries suggest, in fact, that they could, and do, have strong anti-democratic proclivities (Mamdani and Wamba-dia-Wamba, 1995; Mkandawire, 1996).

The Radical Political Economy School

Against the neo-liberal "political economy"/public choice school, most radical political economists contend that structural adjustment and democratic governance are not necessarily or even essentially compatible. This position is arrived at and argued at different levels by different authors working within the broad radical political economy school (Gibbon *et al.*, 1992). At one level, it is premised on the essentially repressive thrust of the adjustment package itself in an analytic frame in which authoritarianism is seen and treated as a property that inheres in the neo-liberal reform model. At another level, the view is argued that structural adjustment, given its unpopularity in many African countries and its failure to deliver quick and tangible benefits, intensifies the authoritarianism that has always been a property of the state in colonial and post-colonial Africa.

Furthermore, there are those who establish the structural adjustment-authoritarianism linkage by focusing on the political strategies of the IMF and the World Bank in the early years of adjustment implementation in Africa, strategies which, according to them, exposed

18

an unmistakable initial/persistent preference by the international financial institutions for authoritarian regimes which were thought to be more capable of taming resistance to the market-based reform measures. In some cases, these authoritarian regimes used the additional resources that adjustment implementation provided to resist or thwart domestic pressures for democratisation. Of course, there are many instances in which the different levels of analyses overlap and the synthesis which follows does not, for the purposes of this study, separate them.

According to many of the radical political economists, the neo-liberal doctrine, the goals which it seeks to achieve, and instruments by which they are to be achieved all carry a repressive load that is directed against a range of local social forces opposed to it, including especially the middle class of professionals and the working/unemployed poor. These forces are often defined in the neo-liberal model as the selfish and self-serving "urban parasites" on whose behalf an inefficient economic order that is biased against the rural poor and the denizens of the informal sector was erected in much of Africa. This way, the repression of opposition, mostly urban-based, to the adjustment project is justified ideologically.

Yet, opposition to structural adjustment is inevitable because all over Africa, its implementation has entailed the imposition of additional economic burdens on the working people and the poor through the devaluation of currencies, the freezing of wages and salaries, massive public sector retrenchments, the imposition of so-called cost recovery measures in the educational and health sectors, the elimination of subsidies (real and invented), the curtailment of the welfare and social expenditure of the state and the high inflationary consequences of price deregulation and rapid devaluation, among others. These are measures which are unpopular in their own right; they are made even more so by the fact that they come as an external imposition implemented by regimes whose legitimacy is, more often than not, in tatters.

The implementation of adjustment measures has often been accompanied by attempts at undermining the organisational capacity and autonomy of the opponents of the adjustment package. This is all the more so as opposition to the adjustment process gathers a nationalist momentum and the state is unable to show tangible results from the "pains" of adjustment either in the short- or long-term. Since a majority of the peoples of the adjusting countries are "losers" from the adjustment process, no significant constituency is able to emerge to make the case for the reform package against its opponents. It is left to state officials, faced with donor conditionality, to attempt to force through the programme and, in doing so, silence the critics administratively.

Resistance to structural adjustment is, however, not limited just to the working poor; it includes significant sections of the middle class, especially the professionals, and the many members of the manufacturing class whose interests are adversely affected by the programme. Attempts at silencing the opposition therefore translate into widespread repression and high-handedness executed by officials representing a contested state. In the view of the radical political economists therefore, authoritarianism rather than democracy is the flipside of structural adjustment implementation in Africa. Being economically repressive, the programme requires an equally politically repressive framework for its implementation. Regimes implementing orthodox structural adjustment not only resort to undemocratic methods of pushing it through, they also make spirited efforts to prevent autonomous organisation for alternatives to the neo-liberal project. The authoritarian import of the adjustment model and the repressiveness associated with its implementation are reinforced by the undemocratic logic and practice of donor conditionality (Bangura 1986, 1989a, 1989b; Hutchful, 1987; Mustapha, 1988, 1992; Campbell, 1989; Ibrahim, 1989, 1990; Beckman, 1990, 1992; Bangura and Beckman, 1991; Gibbon et al., 1992; Olukoshi 1991, 1992; Mamdani, 1991; Mkandawire, 1991, 1996; Nyang'oro and Shaw, 1992; Mkandawire and Olukoshi, 1995).

According to some of the radical political economists, it is the process of organisation of resistance to the authoritarianism and repression associated with structural adjustment implementation that begins to open up (new) democratic possibilities based on the self-organisation of groups opposed to the programme and in spite of state repressiveness. If, therefore, the period of implementation of structural adjustment has witnessed the growth of democratic pressures in many African countries as evidenced by the public demonstrations for political change in all the four corners of the continent, it is not because of structural adjustment *qua* structural adjustment but in spite of it. In their bid to protect themselves against the repressive economic content and political repercussions of structural adjustment, various groups adversely affected by the programme, and whose organised resistance at the trade union, students union and professional association level the state attempted to prevent, had no option but to bear the flag of democratisation and the freedom of association.

The emergence of open resistance to authoritarian rule during the adjustment years was aided by the wave of "democratisation" that swept through the former Soviet bloc and the extremely limited achievement of the market-based economic reform policies themselves. Yet, those countries of Africa where transitions have recently been made to elected forms of government, compelled as they have been under the prevailing international regime to stick to orthodox structural adjustment, are finding that their fragile "democracies" are in peril precisely because of their persistence with an adjustment process that continues to be marked by poor economic results and huge social costs. In many of these countries, the forces in the forefront of the democracy campaign were also quite vociferous in their opposition to IMF/World Bank structural adjustment. These "choiceless democracies", as Mkandawire (1996) describes them, are imperilled by the fact of their being trapped in an unpopular neo-liberal net that appears to be leading nowhere as far as economic growth and development are concerned even as they carry large social costs.

On balance, the insights that emanate from the perspectives of the radical political economy school appear to be far closer to reality in much of Africa than the positions conveyed by the neo-liberal "political economy"/public choice theorists. However, in criticism of the radical political economists, it has been argued that their approach more accurately captures the authoritarian outcomes of adjustment implementation in countries with strong civil societies but is less helpful in understanding the political dynamics in countries with weak or non-existent civil societies. In the latter case, exemplified by Tanzania and Mozambique, a process of "democratisation from above", which is tied to attempts at legitimating a new development strategy favouring private accumulation with state resources and discarding all developmentalist and welfarist pretences, is one possible outcome which many of the radical political economists would seem to rule out *ab initio* (Gibbon, 1992).

It has also been argued, in the light of the contemporary experience in Africa whereby several elected governments are sticking to orthodox adjustment policies, that a more interesting issue to focus on is not whether adjustment and democracy can occur simultaneously and/or co-exist but "... what the dual pursuit of adjustment and democratisation implies for the consolidation of each other, and more specifically for the immediate future of the democratisation process" (Mkandawire, 1996:28). This, of course, does not rule out the possibility, as indeed several scholars have concluded, that continued implementation of orthodox adjustment might adversely affect the consolidation of efforts at political reform in African countries where multi-party elections have been held (Olukoshi, 1995; Mkandawire, 1996).

Donor Parameters and Prescriptions for "Good" Governance in Africa

Diagnosing the African Crisis of Governance

We have already noted that much of the perspective which the donor community, especially the World Bank, brought to bear on its governance work was heavily informed by the output of the public choice school. In many respects, the World Bank, given the resources at its disposal and its wide reach, came to set the pace for other donors, including many of the bilaterals, on the governance question. That being the case, our discussion here of the parameters and prescriptions for the Africa governance programmes of the donors will draw primarily, though not entirely exclusively, on the perspectives and policies which the World Bank developed and has tried to apply in relation to the countries of the continent. This is done without prejudice to the slight differences in definition and emphasis which exist among the donors (see Box 1). For the Bank itself, governance is defined as "... the manner in which power is exercised in the management of a country's economic and social resources for development" (World Bank, 1992:52).

Once it formally joined the governance bandwagon in 1989, the World Bank was to quickly immerse itself in the task of operationalising the term for its own objectives. For this purpose, the 1989 report of the Bank entitled *Sub-Saharan Africa: From Crisis to Sustainable Growth* served as a launching pad. Its diagnosis of the governance-development matrix in Africa more or less replicated the main positions of the public choice approach. According to the Bank, at the heart of the litany of Africa's development problems is a fundamental crisis of governance. This has manifested itself not only in terms of a relentless decline in the quality of government, growing bureaucratic obstruction, and weakened judicial systems, but also in increasing political and administrative arbitrariness, the collapse of the rule of law, and an all-pervasive culture of corruption and rent-seeking. In most African countries, "a deep political malaise" stymies all developmental action. The situation is complicated by the increasing lack of local "capacity" both in the public and private sectors (World Bank, 1989, 1990, 1992, 1994a, 1994b; Nunberg and Nellis, 1990; Landell-

Box 1: Donor definitions of governance

The World Bank's attempts at defining and operationalising governance has led it to identify a number of distinct parts to the concept, namely, the form of political regime in a given country, the process by which authority is exercised in the management of a country's economic and social resources for development, the framework of laws, the structure of accountability, and the capacity of governments to design, formulate, and implement policies and discharge functions.Other multilateral financial institutions more or less adopt the Bank's definition although the Inter-American Development Bank places emphasis on the modernisation of public administration in its own work. For its part, the African Development Bank (ADB) distinguishes between what it describes as macro-, meso-, and micro-governance corresponding to conditions at the upper, middle and lower levels of government. With this formulation, the ADB is able to argue that an authoritarian regime committed to development could, in fact, exhibit "good" governance at the middle and lower levels. Among bilateral donors, their definition of "good" governance links the World Bank's usage of the concept to issues of respect for human/minority rights, the licensing of a free (private) press, and the inauguration of multi-party forms of electoral politics. For this purpose, several Western governments have devised "political conditionality" as an instrument in their relations with the countries of Africa.

Source: Adapted from World Bank, 1994a, p. xiv.

Mills, 1992; Landell-Mills and Serageldin, 1991; Wai, 1991, 1994; Dia, 1993, 1996; Adamolekun and Bryant, 1994).

According to the Bank, soon after independence in Africa, the civil service in most countries not only became overbloated but was also politicised and came to be staffed by inexperienced people brought in through patron-clientelist networks. In time, as the agencies and organisations of government proliferated, the civil service wage bill ballooned, claiming an increasingly disproportionate share of governmental revenues and the national GDP until many countries came to find it difficult even to pay wages and salaries regularly, if at all. The rapid expansion of the public sector wage bill not only created serious fiscal problems but also had the effect of "crowding out" other critical items of current expenditure, especially the maintenance of physical infrastructure and the procurement of essential supplies and equipment. Thus it was that the widespread situation was created where, among other examples, doctors and nurses lacked basic medicines and equipment with which to treat patients, teachers lacked chalk and books for teaching, and postal workers had no stamps and money orders to sell. The decline in motivation that resulted from this situation only reinforced the diminishing productivity of the civil service, a development not helped by the uncompetitive remuneration of those in the management cadre (World Bank, 1989, 1992; Nunberg, 1989; Dia, 1993; Adamolekun and Bryant, 1994; Lindauer and Nunberg, 1996).

Given the host of problems that bedevilled it, it is not surprising that the post-colonial African bureaucracy found it hard to cope with the stresses of "rapid modernisation", a task made more daunting by the embrace by Africa's independence political leaders of "inappropriate" and "ill-adapted" developmental models that were built on Northern values, institutions, and technology.[6] These developmental models, like the state itself, were poorly rooted in African societies, including their history and culture. The state took on the dominant role in the economy partly because of its distrust for private, especially foreign, business and partly to enable it to gain access to resources with which to pamper an "urban coalition" of interests from which its officials were largely recruited. Whatever existed by way of private enterprise was rendered uncompetitive by the heavy costs imposed on it by the degradation of state-maintained physical infrastructure, the breakdown of other basic public functions, red tape, and corruption. The entire political environment was not one which inspired confidence in private investors (World Bank, 1989, 1990, 1992; 1994a, 1994b, Dia, 1993, 1996; Lindauer and Nunberg, 1996).

Elaborating on the Bank's perspective on the crisis of governance in Africa and the ways in which it has stifled development generally, its President, Barber Conable (1991:3), noted that:

> ... All too often, there is a lack of government accountability to the governed, a lack of encouragement that would liberate entrepreneurial instincts, and a general lack of fair competition between farmers and firm.

He added that in much of Africa,

> Open political participation has been restricted and even condemned, and those brave enough to speak their minds have too frequently taken grave personal risks. I fear that many of Africa's leaders have been more concerned about retaining power than about the long-term interests of their people.

The political and other costs of Africa's record of poor governance are, according to the World Bank, legion. Conable, in taking stock of some of those costs, stated that

> ... The political uncertainty and arbitrariness evident in so many parts of sub-Saharan Africa are major constraints on the region's development. Investors will not take risks, entrepreneurs will not be creative, people will not participate if they feel they are facing a capricious, unjust or hostile political environment.

Elaborating further, Conable argued that

> ... Patronage and negotiation have thwarted the formation of professional cadres. Investment in human resource development has lacked direction and commitment. Such practices are a direct cause of Africa's economic growth rate failing in the 1980s to keep pace with population growth, of the debilitating brain drain from the region, and of the extra-ordinary fact that there are more expatriate advisers in Africa today than there were at the end of the colonial period.

The Principles and Parameters for a Solution to Africa's Governance Crisis

Based on its diagnosis of the sources and nature of Africa's crisis of governance, the World Bank proceeded to outline general prescriptions for a solution. The central focus of the prescriptions is a quest for the restructuring of the post-colonial African state in order to make it more supportive of the Bank's long-term strategy for liberating the forces of the market and promoting private enterprise (Beckman, 1992). The Bank had no doubt that there is an organic linkage between the institution of a system of "good" governance and the prospects for the successful implementation of structural adjustment. By encouraging the rule of the impersonal forces of the market and instituting economic "rationality" into the process of resource allocation, a system of open and accountable government would be encouraged. The nurturing of open and transparent governance will, in turn, make it difficult to justify "irrational" economic decisions. For this purpose, the trimming down of the state and its re-orientation away from being an entrepreneur to being a promoter of the private sector remained a central objective. The achievement of this objective was expected to have a "liberating" effect on civil society. It would also result in the "empowerment" of the people. Furthermore, Africa should follow, rather than resist, "... the world-wide trend towards privatisation" (World Bank, 1989:55).

In specifying the elements that were thought to be essential for the attainment of "good" governance in Africa, Bank staff identified the following key principles and parameters (see also Box 2): greater accountability (financial and political) by public officials, including politicians and civil servants; transparency in governmental procedures and processes; a concerted attack on corruption; predictability in governmental behaviour and in the political system; rationality in governmental decisions; competent auditing of governmental transactions; the drastic curbing of bureaucratic red tape; elimination of "unnecessary" administrative controls in order to plug avenues for rent-seeking; the promotion of the free flow of information; the encouragement of a culture of public debate; the institution of a system of checks and balances within the governmental structure; the decentralisation of government; respect for human rights; judicial autonomy and the rule of law; the establishment of a reliable legal framework; and the protection of property and enforcement of contracts. Bank officials also add the issue of capacity-building to enable African technocrats to initiate and implement market-based economic reforms as an essential element of the quest for "good" governance in Africa.

Other donors, particularly the main Western governments and their aid agencies, explicitly advocated and attempted to implement a "new" political conditionality linking aid and other official resource flows to Africa to respect for human rights and the implementation of "democratic" reforms by African governments. As stated by Douglas Hurd (British High Commission, Lagos, 1990:1), British Foreign Secretary until 1995, "... the relief of poverty, hunger, and disease is one of the main tasks of overseas aid. Aid must go where it can clearly do good". He stated further that "Countries tending towards pluralism, public accountability, respect for the rule of law, human rights and market principles should be encouraged. Those who persist with repressive policies, with corrupt management, or with wasteful and discredited economic systems should not expect us to support them with scarce aid resources which could be better used elsewhere".

In essence, for the leading donor countries, democracy, defined in terms of multi-partyism, elections and public accountability, had become the flip side of the neo-liberal market reform project in Africa. Where the Bank couched its political intervention in the affairs of African countries in governance terms that enabled it to claim not to have preferences for particular regime types, the bilateral donors felt no such inhibition and through political conditionality attempted to specify political forms for African countries.

Box 2: Quantification of some governance issues in the World Bank's operations

In 1994, the World Bank published a summary of some of the quantifiable aspects of the governance component of its operations based on aggregated data covering 455 projects in Africa, Asia and Latin America over the period 1991 to 1993. Although serious methodological reservations can be raised about the exercise, it is still useful to reproduce the categories used and percentages arrived at in order to offer a further insight into the parameters used by the Bank in its bid to operationalise the governance concept.

Category	Proportion of lending operations with governance content (per cent)
Legal Framework	6
Participation	30
State-Owned Enterprises Reform	33
Economic Management	49
Capacity Building	68
Decentralisation	68

Source: World Bank, 1994a, p. xv.

Operationalising the Principles and Parameters for "Good" Governance

In attempting to give operational content to its vision of a system of governance in Africa that is supportive of its reform project on the continent, the World Bank embarked on the articulation and implementation of a host of policy measures either on its own or in collaboration with other (mostly smaller, bilateral donors) and multilateral agencies of the United Nations (see Box 2). At one level, this involved the intensification of efforts at securing the implementation of existing Bank and Fund policies that were thought to be relevant to the governance agenda. In this regard, public enterprise privatisation and the reform of the civil/public service were pursued with even more vigour. With regard to the latter, the Bank's focus was primarily on cost containment, staff retrenchment, elimination of "ghost workers" from the payroll, equipment provisioning, revision of the civil service code, public financial management reform, decentralisation of government, and efforts at "professionalisation" (World Bank, 1994a, 1994b; Adamolekun and Bryant, 1994; Dia, 1993, 1996; Lindauer and Nunberg, 1996).

As of the end of 1994, the Bank was supporting various civil service reform programmes in 29 African countries, namely, Angola, Benin, Burkina Faso, Cameroon, Central African Republic, Cape Verde, Comoros, Congo, Gabon, The Gambia, Ghana, Guinea, Guinea Bissau, Madagascar, Malawi, Mauritania, Mozambique, Niger, Nigeria, Rwanda, Sao Tomé and Principe, Senegal, Sierra Leone, Sudan, Tanzania, Togo, Uganda, Zaire and Zambia (see Boxes 3 and 4). The quest for public enterprise and civil service reform formed the kernel of the Bank's public sector management programme in Africa during the 1980s and 1990s. At the heart of the programme was a commitment to cost containment which came to be seen as as central to the prospects for the (eventual) creation of an efficient and effective public service as stabilisation is supposed to be to the restoration of economic growth through a package of adjustment measures (Lindauer and Nunberg, 1996).

Beyond the attempts at pushing the privatisation of public enterprises and the reform of the civil service, the Bank also invested in several countries in projects in the area of accounting and auditing as part of its stated goal of improving financial accountability in the public sector, including support, as in the case of Zambia, to the Public Accounts Committee of the Parliament. Public expenditure reviews became a regular feature of discussions between Bank officials and African governments, with the former aiming to directly influence the expenditure outlays of the latter within and among sectors. Open competitive tendering for contracts and the organisation of competition in service delivery were also undertaken in a number of countries. In this regard, the Bank's country procurement assessment reviews were used to try to influence the practices of various governments as were the financial accountability assessments undertaken in Ghana and South Africa.

Furthermore, attempts were made to set up public works agencies outside the governmental structure and to introduce what is described as "beneficiary participation" in the design of projects. Private sector groups were surveyed with a view to identifying aspects of the civil service and/or its operations that might be reformed to better serve the goal of creating an environment conducive to investors. One outcome of this was the introduction by many countries of "one-stop" investment advisory, vetting, and approval centres that were expected to cut the bureaucratic red tape—and corruption associated with the procurement of governmental approval for proposed investment projects (World Bank, 1994a, 1994b; Adamolekun and Bryant, 1994; Dia, 1996).

Box 3: Components of the main civil service reforms implemented in various sub-Saharan African countries in the period to the end of 1991 as built into the World Bank's SALs, TALs, and ERPs*

Studies/
diagnostics

Angola
Benin
Burkina Faso
Cent. Afr. Rep.
Gabon
Ghana
Guinea
Mali
Mauritania
Mozambique
Niger
Rwanda
Senegal
Togo

Civil service surveys/
head counts/functional
reviews

Benin
Cent. Afr. Rep.
Comoros
Congo
Gambia, The
Ghana
Guinea
Guinea-Bissau
Mauritania
Rwanda
Senegal
Uganda
Zambia

Data collection/
mechanisation of
management duties

Benin
Burkina Faso
Cent. Afr. Rep.
Comoros
Gabon
Ghana
Mali
Mauritania
Senegal
Togo
Uganda

Training (locally
and abroad)

Angola
Benin
Gabon
Ghana
Guinea
Madagascar
Malawi
Mali
Mauritania
Mozambique
Niger
Rwanda
Senegal
Uganda
Zambia

Wage and salary freezes
and cuts, decompression
and grading

Benin
Burkina Faso
Cameroon
Cent. Afr. Rep.
Congo
Gabon
Gambia, The
Ghana
Guinea
Mali
Mauritania
Mozambique
Niger
Sao Tomé & P.
Senegal
Togo
Uganda
Zaire

Staff reductions/employ-
ment freezes/enforcement
of early retirement age

Benin
Cameroon
Cent. Afr. R.
Comoros
Congo
Gabon
Gambia, The
Ghana
Guinea
Guinea Bissau
Mauritania
Niger
Sao Tomé & P.
Senegal
Uganda
Zambia

Voluntary departure/
severance

Benin
Cameroon
Cent. Afr. Rep.
Comoros
Congo
Gambia, The
Ghana
Guinea
Guinea Bissau
Mali
Mauritania
Senegal

Creation/strengthening of
personnel management institutions

Benin
Central Africa Republic
Comoros
Gambia, The
Ghana
Guinea
Mali
Mauritania
Sao Tomé & Principe
Senegal
Togo
Uganda

*SALs: Structural Adjustment Loans;
TALs: Technical Adjustment Loans;
ERPs: Economic Recovery Programmes
Source: Adapted from Lindauer and Nunberg (1996), pp. 126–127

Box 4: The Nigerian civil service reforms

The Nigerian structural adjustment programme started in 1986/1987 shortly after the coming to power of General Ibrahim Babangida through a palace *coup d'état* that took place in August, 1985. One important component of the programme was the decision by the government, under advice from the World Bank, to undertake a sweeping reform of the civil service. For this purpose, a committee was set up, under the chairmanship of Professor Adedotun Phillips, to make recommendations to the government on the options that were available and the steps that it was necessary to undertake.

Following the submission of the report of the Phillips committee, the government decided, among other things, to "professionalise" the civil service through a scheme whereby officers would work in ministries appropriate to their training and develop their career on this basis. New titles for some categories of work were introduced as part of the effort to "streamline" and apply the new principle of professionalism. It was also decided that productivity, merit and competence would prevail over seniority and tenure in the assessment of staff performance. Automaticity in the promotion of staff was to be abandoned too. Furthermore, the post of the permanent secretary as the most senior civil servant and accounting officer in any given ministry was abolished and replaced with politically-appointed directors-general who, unlike the permanent secretaries of old, would leave office with the regime that appointed them.

Under this scheme, ministers became the chief accounting officers for the ministries over which they presided. A revamped Federal Civil Service Commission was to play an enlarged role in the appointment, training, and disciplining of staff. Also as part of this reform process, the Central Bank of Nigeria was removed from the supervisory purview of the Federal Ministry of Finance and placed under the Presidency.

But the view among most students of Nigerian public administration is that the reforms, far from stemming the decline of the civil service, actually accelerated it by weakening internal mechanisms of accountability/checks and balances through the politicisation of the position of the permanent secretary/director-general and the vesting of powers of financial administration and accounting in the hands of ministers. Several ministries were paralysed by conflicts between ministers and their directors-general over matters of procedure and control of resources. Partly to enable them to over-ride internal procedures and manage "opposition" within the bureaucracy, ministers recruited and relied heavily on "special assistants", basically ministerial political appointees brought in from outside the civil service system.

The collapse of morale continued unrestrained, exacerbated by the failure to stem the unrelenting decline in public sector real income as the Nigerian currency, the Naira, fell freely at the official foreign exchange auction and on the parallel market. Discipline broke down and corruption remained rampant.

In 1994, the military government of General Sani Abacha decided to abandon an important aspect of the reforms by reverting directors-general back to the status of career civil servants who will not be required to leave office with the government that appointed them.

Source: Author's fieldwork

In the area of enhancing the rule of law, the Bank concentrated most of its attention on ways by which legal institutions in Africa could be strengthened and "outdated" laws reformed. One of the underlying assumptions informing the Bank's work in this regard is the view that an "appropriate" legal system is necessary for stability and predictability. As part of its strategy, the Bank pushed for specific reforms in Angola, Cape Verde, Côte d'Ivoire, Ghana, Guinea, Mali, and Uganda aimed at re-orienting the legal regime more explicitly and "efficiently" in support of property rights and contracts as they affect private sector loans and credits.

Projects focusing on legal training (targeted mainly at legal draftsmen) and the renovation/development of court infrastructure were also earmarked for execution in Burkina Faso, Mozambique, Tanzania, and Zambia. Furthermore, the Bank's Africa region, through its Women in Development (WID) unit, sponsored several studies and workshops on legal constraints affecting the "economic empowerment" of women. Within this framework, it established links with national legal associations and law-related research groups in various countries as strategic entry points for the Bank's legal reform work, both generally and in relation to women (World Bank, 1994b).

In addition to measures such as the promotion of open, competitive tendering for the supply of goods and services to the government by the private sector, including NGOs, the Bank sought to improve transparency in the governmental process by encouraging several African countries to publish official gazettes advertising public tenders and announcing their award. Burkina Faso and Mauritania are just two of the several countries where this strategy was pushed through. Governments were also encouraged, as in Kenya, to publish a summary version of their annual budget plans for circulation locally. This practice was expected to stimulate public debate on the economy and the public expenditure pattern adopted by the incumbent regime. In a bid to encourage "informed" reporting and public discussion of economic reform issues, the Bank's Economic Development Institute (EDI) developed training programmes for journalists invited from time to time from various African countries. Publications from the Bank were also routinely targeted at the media in all of the adjusting countries of Africa and briefing sessions regularly scheduled to "explain" the objectives of the economic reform process, the successes recorded and the problems that persist (World Bank, 1994a).

The Bank's work in the area of institution-building was extended, in principle and in practice, to support for non-governmental/ "grassroots" organisations. These organisations are seen as viable replacements for the state in several spheres; they are also central to the Bank's strategy for "empowering" the people and "thickening" civil society as a counterweight to the "(neo-)patrimonial" state. Not only was the establishment of NGOs/"grassroots" organisations explicitly encouraged in various African countries, attempts were also made to make them beneficiaries of procurement contracts awarded by the state and project funds supplied by donors, including the Bank. Indeed, in several countries, the Bank inspired the establishment of NGOs for the execution of public works projects. The experiences of the Hometown Associations (HTAs) of West Africa were also studied with a view to replicating them in other parts of the continent as part of the quest for the expansion of NGO involvement in community development (World Bank, 1989, 1992, 1994a; Landell-Mills, 1992).

Also central to the governance programme of the Bank in Africa is "capacity building" in the public and private sectors. The Bank's work in this area was premised on the assumption that a key element in the African crisis is the absence or collapse of "effective" policy-making and managerial capacity that is both up to date and relevant to the changing international economic environment in general and the promotion of market-based reform in particular. Indeed, for the Bank, capacity-building came to be regarded as yet another "missing link" in Africa's quest for development. That being so, the donor community, led by the Bank, invested resources in programmes and projects aimed at building capacity on the continent. In 1991, several donors came together to establish an Africa Capacity Building Foundation (ACBF) in Harare, Zimbabwe.

Various forms of "technical" and "institutional" assistance were offered to different African governments to upgrade skills, improve procedures, strengthen organisation, and encourage the more effective utilisation of existing skills and assets, especially in the management of market-based reforms. NGOs and private sector agencies were important beneficiaries of the capacity building efforts of the donors, with the ACBF playing an important role in this regard. The goal of building capacity was complemented by another project, championed by the United Nations Development Programme (UNDP), ostensibly to retain talent in Africa and stem/reverse the brain drain from the continent (World Bank, 1991; Dia, 1996). An associated objective of capacity building, partly also serving as a justification for it, was the promotion of local "ownership" of the donor adjustment model.

Furthermore, as part and parcel of the governance-adjustment linkage of the Bank, school curricula, especially at the tertiary level, were brought under scrutiny and recommendations made for course/departmental rationalisation. As with the reforms of the civil service, the claim was that the educational sector reforms proposed by the Bank will make African tertiary education more "relevant" and result-oriented, not to speak of cost effective. The staff-student ratio in many countries was brought under scrutiny and proposals for cost recovery on many of the services provided by schools were presented. The administrative structure of higher educational institutions also came under close scrutiny and reform proposals were outlined. Loans were made available to governments for the re-equipping of laboratories and libraries and the rehabilitation of physical infrastructure within the overall framework of the rationalisation plans that the Bank advocated and the implementation targets which governments accepted.

Also, there was the claim that the reduction of the number of universities/polytechnics will help to channel resources to intermediate level technical manpower development which is lacking in much of Africa. Such rationalisation might also enable resources to be freed for support to the primary education sector. The re-organisation of university curricula should also enable governments to de-emphasise the liberal arts and strengthen the technical and engineering services. A closer linkage between the educational sector and the private sector was also advocated by the Bank as part of the reform agenda. This way, not only would universities be able to attract some private sector funding, but the training of human resources would also be more closely linked to the demands of the market generally and the labour market in particular.[7]

Apart from the specific ideological-political load which the donor brand of governance carries, it is worth remarking that during the 1980s and early 1990s, there was a clear preference expressed for the insertion of technocrats in the political and administrative structures and processes of African countries, and their elevation to a high profile as part of the "good" governance-efficient adjustment implementation linkage. Where it was assumed that Africa's "old guard" patrimonial rulers were less inclined to faithfully implement structural adjustment because of its potential for undermining the clientelist networks on which their personal rule rested, the technocrats were thought to be driven purely by considerations of competence and professionalism required for effective reform implementation.

Thus, in various African countries, most notably Benin, Côte d'Ivoire, Nigeria, Senegal, and Togo, technocrats either took over some of the highest political offices or were placed in strategic ministries at the heart of government. In less evident or celebrated cases,

Box 5: African technocrats and the adjustment process

During the adjustment years of the 1980s and 1990s, various African governments were encouraged to appoint and/or promote technocrats into positions of responsibility in the expectation that this would produce greater commitment to the reform process, restore (foreign) investor confidence in the economy, and create an altogether better administrative/political environment for the implementation of market-based reforms.

Thus, in Senegal, Abdou Diouf who succeeded Sedar Senghor to the presidency brought in a team of technocrats, vested with numerous powers and privileges, to carry out the country's economic reform programme.

In Nigeria, the military regime of General Ibrahim Babangida which, in 1986, ended the stalemate between the country and the Bretton Woods twins over an appropriate adjustment package for the country appointed as Finance Minister, a US-based economist, Kalu Idika Kalu, who had once worked for the World Bank (and was once a resident adviser at the Bank's mission in South Korea) and as National Planning Minister, another US-based economist, Chu S.P. Okongwu, who had trained at Harvard and had links with the leading multilateral financial institutions.

In Zimbabwe, Robert Mugabe was prevailed upon to entrust the implementation of his government's economic reform programme to that "technocrat of technocrats", Bernard Chidzero who was well known internationally and had "excellent connections" with the IMF and the World Bank.

In the case of Côte d'Ivoire, the late President Houphouet Boigny was leaned upon to bring in Alassane Ouattara, deputy managing director of the IMF and one-time Governor of the Banque Centrale des États de l'Afrique de l'Ouest (BCEAO), as his Prime Minister with full responsibility for economic matters. Ouattara, in turn, appointed a former BCEAO colleague of his, Kablan Duncan, as Finance Minister. Following Konan Bedié's triumph, with backing from Paris, over Ouattara in the struggle to succeed Houphouet Boigny after his death, Duncan was elevated to the post of Prime Minister and yet another old BCEAO hand was named Finance Minister.

In Burkina Faso and Niger, the incumbent prime ministers are old BCEAO hands. In Benin Republic, a former World Bank employee, Nicephore Soglo, served as President of the country until his defeat in the elections that were held in March 1996.

The examples are endless and they point to the ascendancy of a technocracy in a process that fitted well into the donor governance strategy for the continent. Yet, in many cases, partly because of their lack of political and bureaucratic experience and partly because they did not know the local terrain well, having, in some instances, been away from home for prolonged periods, their presence failed to have the decisive impact that was expected. Matters were not helped by the image of detached arrogance that followed them in the public eye. The fact that many of them were not inclined to recognise the political limitations of their policies and failed to develop a system of consultation with key social actors also helped to undermine them.

In several cases, some of the technocrats either fell from power (Soglo in Benin is probably the most spectacular recent example), were unable to win seats in local elections (the Senegalese experience is salutary in this regard) or were simply shoved aside into inconsequential positions (as became the lot of Kalu Idika Kalu in Nigeria). Those who remained in office did so largely by the grace of the politicians who appointed them and whose interests they had now learned to accommodate. Interestingly, a factor in Soglo's defeat in the Benin elections was the widespread perception that he ran a corrupt and nepotistic regime that, at the very least, showed that he and his team were not that different from the *ancien regime* they replaced.

Sources: Author's survey; Diop and Diouf, 1990; Bangura, 1994b; Ka and van de Walle 1994; Mkandawire, 1996.

technocrats, including nationals of some of the African countries concerned, were seconded to the national bureaucracy, especially the economic ministries, whilst keeping their international pay/perks (see Box 5). Questions of how these technocrats might be "insulated" from untoward advances and pressures from local interests formed a key element in the discourse of the public choice theorists. Such then, was the thrust of the donor governance programme. It is a programme that has been subjected to extensive criticism as much over its content as over its ideological-political fabric and context and its coupling to the neo-liberal economic adjustment project. Let us now proceed to elaborate on some of the criticisms.

Structural Adjustment and Governance in Africa
—The Pitfalls of the Donor Approach

The point should be stressed at this stage that at the heart of the concern in the donor community generally, and the World Bank in particular, about questions of governance in Africa is the desire to promote the emergence of a conducive, and in their view, more legitimate political context, backed by the requisite administrative capacity, for the successful implementation of orthodox structural adjustment. In this thinking, the very adjustment model which is being pushed is hardly problematised. The possibility that the implementation of that model may, in fact, feed into and exacerbate Africa's governance problems is, therefore, ignored. All of the Bank's investment in political theory is, thus, primarily designed to find political supporting blocks for orthodox adjustment to be more "effectively" implemented.

Yet, policy and its implementation are always the objects of contestation among different forces in every political system. It is never clear, however, why in the case of Africa, the Bank and its governance theorists consider this not to be applicable, and where it is acknowledged, to treat it as *solely,* or even *primarily,* the result of the "selfish" and "illegitimate" machinations of "vested interests" that are steeped in a variety of "(neo-) patrimonial" relations. In this fundamental sense, the donor governance programme amounts to little more than an attempt to "save" an adjustment model that has been a source of intense controversy and contestation. In doing this, the Bank has adopted an approach which, at one level, pretends that opposition to adjustment is either absent or is not fundamental. At another level, it has sought to selectively co-opt the language and some aspects of the platform of the forces which have articulated and led opposition to structural adjustment and the authoritarian state in Africa. This way, a decisive ideological-political attempt is made to neutralise the opposition.

Although the language of the Bank's governance discourse ("civil society", "accountability", "empowerment", "rule of law", "popular participation", etc) is one which, on the face of things, fits into the renewed global interest in issues of democracy, the governance programme is, in fact, reduced to a managerial/technocratic affair tailored to the goals of an adjustment programme that, in the view of many, has, at the very least, contributed to the reproduction/ intensification of authoritarianism in Africa. The question of *democratic governance* in Africa is, therefore, one which is still unresolved. This is without prejudice to the fact that there has been some association in the Bank literature, and in the writings of some its intellectual supporters, between governance and "democracy" (World Bank, 1994b).

The question of democratic governance also goes beyond the inauguration of an elected government dedicated to the pursuit of unpopular economic reforms that are the product of an external imposition and which exact huge costs without showing tangible results.[8] In the end, the challenge of democratic governance is the reality that some of the main bearers of the struggle for democracy in Africa are also in the frontline of the resistance to structural adjustment implementation. Many of them have sharpened their strategies for the democratisation of their societies from their experience of resisting the authoritarian practices predating, but reinforced by, the implementation of structural adjustment. The concerns and interests of the various forces in society, not least those of the opposition to structural adjustment, will have to be taken much more seriously in a political governance framework which does not foreclose discussion on the economic reform model that will be adopted.

Taking stock of the governance agenda of the Bank, Beckman, in one of the most powerful published critiques of its 1989 report, persuasively argued that the institution's intervention in that arena seeks to boost state capacity for orthodox adjustment implementation not by addressing the objections of those opposed to the programme but by seeking to undercut their political and ideological legitimacy. This is done partly by feigning a consensus that does not exist and partly by the promise of a better, rosier tomorrow that may never come but which helps to shift focus away from the current practice and consequences of structural adjustment. But much more fundamentally, the Bank attempts to blunt and discredit the extensive and powerful reservoir of nationalist opposition to structural adjustment as a foreign imposition by dismissing the forces of nationalism as being, historically, the peddlers in post-independence Africa of "inappropriate" ideas of modernisation borrowed uncritically from abroad.

In developing this line of attack, not only does the Bank resort to a systematic distortion of the post-colonial developmental experience (for example, the claim that most governments drew up "comprehensive five year plans" and invested in "large, state-run *core* industries" which is contrary to the empirical evidence), but it also attempts to distance itself from developmental objectives and strategies (for example, support for state development finance companies set up to act as "trustees" for the emerging private sector) with which it was ideologically and financially involved. Furthermore, the Bank's resort to labelling the opponents of its adjustment project as "selfish", "narrow" and "urban-based" sidesteps the reality that the allegedly "narrow" interests which organised interest groups in much of Africa convey appeal to wider popular aspirations that strike a chord with various groups in urban as well as rural areas (Beckman, 1992).

For Beckman, as for other critics, the governance programme of the Bank is also aimed at establishing an alternative basis of popular legitimacy for structural adjustment. That is why notions such as "grassroots empowerment", "mobilisation", "civil society", "equity", and "participation" have been central to its governance discourse. But at the hands of the Bank, the political-democratic side of these concepts are downplayed and their technocratic-managerial ones played up. Thus, for example, in the Bank's "political economy", "empowerment" refers, in the main, to freedom for local private entrepreneurs and not to the institutionalisation of popular participation in collective decision-making. Seen from this angle, the donor concern is, therefore, less with democracy and more with "development". "Empowerment", for example, is seen as something to be encouraged insofar as it is considered to be good for "development". The "rule of law" is discussed and operationalised in terms which focus on the creation of a legal framework within which private, mainly foreign business confidence can grow. But such notions of empowerment and the rule of law do not address the concerns of the opponents of the adjustment process who consider themselves as losers in one sense or another. Thus, in the end, the Bank's governance agenda is part of a broader project of managerial populism which does not signal the dawn of a new era of "adjustment with a democratic face" which is able to dovetail into what Mkandawire (1996) has described as "democracy without tears". For, stripped of its rhetoric, the governance programme of the Bank fails to address the question of why the politics of adjustment has been so repressive in Africa (Beckman, 1992).

When the governance positions espoused by the Bank are taken at their face value and squared up with the practice of structural adjustment initiation and implementation, it emerges clearly that there are strong grounds for questioning their compatibility. At one level, attention has been drawn to the fact that the relationship between the donors and African governments, both generally and in the process of adjustment initiation and implementation particularly, is hardly a democratic one. As Mkandawire (1996:35) notes, donor resource flows to Africa have mainly been disbursed "... within essentially authoritarian structures". This institutional reality has been reinforced during the adjustment years through the tightening and intensification of donor conditionality and cross-conditionality, a process aided by the World Bank's heavy investment in the strategy of donor consultation and co-ordination.[9] It has also been reinforced by the *TINA* ("there is no alternative") ideology with which African governments have been confronted at every turn. The logic of conditionality, donor co-ordination and *TINA* compel adjusting governments to embrace a reform project which they may not necessarily believe in and strive to implement it in the face of domestic opposition, popular disaffection, and limited results. It also sidesteps the domestic policy process, further erodes national sovereignty over basic economic policy decision-making, and undermines local policy-making capacity (Beckman, 1992; Stokke, 1995; Mkandawire, 1996; Engberg-Pedersen *et al.*, 1996; Engberg-Pedersen, 1996; Gibbon and Olukoshi, 1996; Olukoshi, 1996).

At another level, the logic and demands of donor conditionality and cross-conditionality have meant that, for all intents and purposes, African governments have increasingly had to devote a good proportion of their time and resources to accounting to donors. Officials are constantly working on reports for the Bank, the Fund, a host of bilateral donors, and the Paris and London clubs. They are also required to spend time with a variety of visiting evaluation/monitoring missions. They too undertake missions of their own to the Bretton Woods institutions, the Paris and London Clubs, and other donors to defend their record and make the case for financing. The net effect of all this is that in many countries, governmental effectiveness has been further impaired even as key economic ministries were brought directly under donor influence. As Gibbon (Gibbon and Olukoshi, 1996) notes, "... the increasing "donorisation" of many branches of government activity ... (added) to ministerial administrative burdens".

The undermining of governmental effectiveness in Africa also reinforced the erosion of the state's political capacity, defined as the "... the ability to construct and maintain a working political coalition capable of sustaining the implementation of state policy" (Beckman, 1992: 95). In the midst of all this, the Bretton Woods twins have taken on the status of "offshore governments" which, for all intents and purposes, control the content and direction of economic and social policy in Africa, exact accountability from African officials to their head offices in Washington, D.C. but strive to avoid taking on a commensurate amount of responsibility for the consequences of the policies whose implementation they enforce (Olukoshi, 1996).

Furthermore, the practice of adjustment implementation in most African countries has hardly conformed with the most elementary norms of "transparency" and "accountability" by rulers to the ruled. From the time discussions about structural adjustment initiation are started, they are shrouded in mystery which officials (both on the donor side and local state side) insist is necessary in view of the "delicate" nature of the negotiations. The local media are suffused with rumours based on information that leaks from the secret negotiations. Newspaper cartoonists attempt to capture the atmosphere of secrecy with images of IMF and World Bank officials wearing dark spectacles arriving in African capitals in the dead of the night and taking the first flight out when dawn breaks. Once the adjustment deal is sealed, another round of secrecy and evasion surrounds its content and the timing and sequencing of its implementation.

As the adjustment policies begin to be sprung on the people, leaders embark on "news management" mostly aimed at limiting the flow of information on the reform programme. Exercises in "data massaging" are undertaken in order to paint a rosier picture of economic performance than is really the case. The language of economic discourse becomes more and more obscure such that the ordinary people tend to be intimidated into silence. As we noted earlier, the officials charged with implementing the unpopular reform programme come to see themselves as being more accountable to the donors who exercise direct leverage over them and not to the populace who bear the brunt of the market reform policies. The entire process is one which does not allow much room for consultation with the people or internal and open policy debates within the governmental system. Indeed, only a tiny elite in the central bank, the office of the president/prime minister and the ministry of finance have a full picture of the entire adjustment package. Others have, at best, only a selective picture. Inter-ministerial co-ordination therefore becomes difficult as does planning on a national scale. Morale among those in the policy apparatus who are excluded becomes low.

Yet, it is not as if, for all of the costs which the market reform project exacts, the structural adjustment years have been marked by a taming of corruption. In fact, the problem of corruption has been deepened in many cases, fuelled by the decline in real income and living standards which has encouraged the intensification of petty graft among some categories of workers as a survival strategy. Among ruling class elements, new forms of "market-driven" corruption have emerged/intensified linked to the entire environment/process of liberalisation generally, and, more specifically, to the privatisation/commercialisation/liquidation of public enterprises, the auctioning of foreign exchange, the floatation of enterprises on local stock exchanges, and the deregulation of interest rates. In Nigeria, the probe of the banking and financial sector which began in 1994 has produced startling evidence of "market-driven" corruption in the period since 1986 when the country's adjustment programme started. Yet, the financial sector deregulation policies of the Nigerian state were once hailed as a hallmark of the "successes" of adjustment in Nigeria. In Kenya, the spectacular fortune illicitly amassed by Nicholas Biwot, once a pillar of the ruling Kenyan African National Union and close confidant of President Daniel Arap Moi, and his cronies was built on a systematic manipulation of the structures and processes of adjustment-related deregulation. Land-related scandals deriving from attempts at privatising what is by far Africa's most important resource have been reported in all corners of the continent. The examples are endless and they suggest that the market is not exactly the anti-corruption antidote that it has been presented to be. Both the public and private sectors continue to be wracked by corruption in much of Africa.

The crisis and adjustment years in Africa have had far-reaching, adverse consequences for the administrative structure and capacity of many countries on the continent which the governance programme of the donors has hardly addressed in a manner that can offer an enduring basis for meaningful renewal. Many civil service organisations have been severely weakened not only by staff retrenchments and the effects of the exercises on the morale of those retained but also by the collapse of the income (and purchasing power) of those employed in the public sector in the face of currency devaluation and massive inflationary pressures. The sharp decline in the real value of civil service pay, even where it was already underway during the pre-adjustment period, was reinforced by the devaluation measures that became the defining feature of the quest for adjustment and the inflationary pressures associated with them (Robinson, 1990). In many countries (see Box 3), wage and salary freezes were also imposed; several countries even carried out cuts in the nominal pay of their civil servants. From being largely competitive with the remuneration available to employees in the local private sector, civil service pay levels in most African countries were, during the adjustment years, to fall way behind what was on offer in the local private sector; they became even less competitive internationally. One consequence of this development is that experienced and qualified personnel have, increasingly, been drained out of the public sector partly into the local private sector but overwhelmingly into the international labour market (see Box 6).

It is important to underline the fact of the collapse of public sector wages and salaries because this is one issue that has been central to the collapse of morale and effectiveness in the public sector. In a sense, the wholesale, one-sided anti-statist ideology on the platform of which the neo-liberal reform project for Africa was inaugurated was one which cast the civil service in bad light and meant that the overall emphasis of the World Bank's reform effort was on cutting it down to size. The centrality of the goal of restoring internal fiscal balances to the donor stabilisation-adjustment programme also meant that there was little room for any serious consideration of the ways in which the pay and purchasing power of civil servants could be enhanced. Thus, the anti-statism of the adjustment package reinforced, and was reinforced by, the demand management, deflationary thrust of the economic reform programme. The focus of attention was, therefore, on cost containment/reduction which, almost always, translated into the retrenchment of workers and the freezing of pay.

Of course, suggestions were made that the savings from the reduction of civil service sizes might be used to enhance the pay of those who remain in public sector employment. But this was more an ideological proposition for legitimating retrenchment rather than a serious strategy for pay review with a view to making the civil service an attractive place within which to make a career. Not surprisingly, the proposition never gathered steam anywhere in Africa. Little wonder then, that the goal of making the civil service more professional, efficient and effective has been undermined by the very adjustment package on the basis of which reform is being pursued.

Faced with diminishing real incomes (and purchasing power) and ever-rising costs of living, many public sector employees have resorted to moonlighting activities in their bid to supplement their wages and salaries. These activities are almost always undertaken during office hours; offices have also been used as informal market outlets for selling a variety of consumer items at a discount. In addition, state resources (personnel, vehicles etc) are sometimes mobilised in support of the multiple livelihood strategies that have become prevalent. The consequences on the effectiveness of the civil service have been telling. It is not surprising that the civil service all over Africa has found it increasingly difficult to attract and retain high calibre local personnel with the requisite experience and expertise. The resultant "capacity gap" has largely been tackled through a resort to the employment of consultants, mostly from abroad.

The use of highly paid "independent" expatriate consultants who are remunerated in foreign currency and at internationally competitive rates to execute specific adjustment-related tasks has not only meant that the issue of the level of pay of local staff is effectively side-stepped but has also bred resentment which has deepened demoralisation and, occasionally, inspired acts of sabotage against the consultants and the adjustment process itself. In the context of all of the foregoing, it is not difficult to understand why there are at present more expatriate "experts" in crisis-ridden Africa than there were at the dawn of independence in the 1960s (Beckman, 1992; Mustapha, 1992; Bangura, 1994a; Mkandawire, 1996; Olukoshi, 1996).

The explicit preference which was to be shown for technocrats, the basic reasons that informed that preference and proposals on how the technocrats might be "insulated" from local influences represent an extension of the concern within the Bank and among some in the public choice school to seek ways of circumventing politics and getting orthodox adjustment policies implemented. In this sense, the preference for technocrats and for their insulation directly contradicts the donor concern with "transparency" and "accountability". It is remarkable that this preference gained in momentum even as the civil services of most African countries were suffering serious problems of de-professionalisation and the collapse of morale. Many of the high pro-

Box 6: "My boss is a comedian. The wages he pays are a joke"

The collapse of public sector pay in structurally-adjusting Africa is symptomatic of the decisive shift in the structure of incentives away from employment in the civil service and most public sector institutions. The rapidity and depth of the collapse in pay is illustrated by the fact that in Nigeria, the cost of a return air ticket between Lagos and London is, roughly, the gross annual pay of a director-general in the civil service, the vice-chancellor and the most senior professors in the universities, the average senior judge in the judicial system, and the highest paid medical professionals in the hospitals. For the overwhelming majority of civil/public service employees who fall outside this category of the most senior personnel, surviving on what passes for a wage/salary is a constant exercise in self-denial that has ensured that they are consigned to the margins of society and a life of bare subsistence.

The Nigerian case may seem dramatic but it is by no means exceptional since the same basic reality obtains in at least 41 other African countries, including Angola, Benin, Burkina Faso, Central African Republic, Guinea, Mali, Mozambique, Sierra Leone, and Zambia, to cite a few examples, where the situation is even worse than in Nigeria.

Relative to the cost of living, civil service/public sector wages and salaries in much of Africa have become derisory and have, partly, spurred a process of international migration whereby professionals, the most internationally competitive category of Africans, have been moving in droves to the Middle East, North America, Europe in search of "greener pastures". But more than this, it has contributed to the growth of a trend whereby African university graduates are moving to other parts of the world to be employed as poorly paid, and often uninsured, labourers in Europe and North America carrying out tasks that have no bearing on their training and are well below their qualifications. Giving its verdict on the pay situation, the Academic Staff Union of Universities of Nigeria which has been entangled in a prolonged struggle with the Nigerian state over this and other related issues stated: "My boss is a comedian. The wages he pays are a joke". It is a statement which many in Africa will identify with very easily.

Source: Author's field survey

file technocrats who were elevated into senior governmental positions saw themselves as owing little responsibility to be accountable locally. This tended to be particularly so where politicians and the public were aware that particular technocrats had the full backing of the international financial institutions, the creditors, the bilaterals, and the "market". In such situations, technocratic accountability is swung decisively in favour of donors and local scrutiny is dismissed, a trend which "insulation", the quest to make technocrats "autonomous" of domestic social forces, tends to reinforce and accentuate (see Box 5).

The adjustment years have also been marked by a further erosion of the legitimacy of the post-colonial African state, with implications for its political capacity to implement policies. The efforts at re-trenching the state not only helped to curb its social reach but also further undermined the post-colonial social contract on the basis of which it sought to construct ideological legitimation, build political alliances, relate to the opposition, and secure the co-operation/support of autonomous centres of power (Beckman, 1992; Olukoshi and Laakso, 1996). Furthermore, the adjustment years have been asso-ciated with the collapse of a pattern of expectations, concretised in specific group and community demands, focused on what the role of the state is understood as being. This collapse of expectations is rein-forced by the widespread awareness that structural adjustment has come to Africa as an external imposition. In the search for alternatives, individuals and groups are driven into ethno-political and religious organisational frameworks that pose direct challenges to the post-colonial secular, national-territorial nation-state project. That is why some commentators have argued that the crisis of governance in Africa is also, in essence, a crisis of structural adjustment (Beckman, 1992; Olukoshi and Laakso, 1996).

In order for democracy and democratic governance to prevail and become consolidated, there must be social groups within various countries that have an interest in them as specific political projects. Yet, ironically, those very social groups that have, historically, been the main bearers of the struggle for the democratisation of the African state, economy, governmental structure, and society are not only among those most adversely affected by structural adjustment but are also rejected in the adjustment model, and by the most influential donors, as "parasites" and "vested interests" to be undermined politi-cally as part of the bid to dislodge the influence of the "urban coali-tion" which allegedly makes "rational" economic policy-making and implementation impossible. These social forces—workers, students, professionals, academics, etc.—and their organisations have been specifically targeted for disorganisation by the ideologues and execu-tioners of the neo-liberal adjustment project. Trade unions, students' organisations, professional associations and other organised groups opposed to structural adjustment have generally been smashed all over Africa or their organisational capacity severely weakened through constant official harassment, proscription, arrests and imprisonments, and staged-managed divisions (Beckman, 1992; Bangura and Beckman, 1991; Mustapha, 1988; Mkandawire and Olukoshi, 1996; Olukoshi, 1996).

The notions of democracy and democratisation which the students, workers, professionals and other groups with an active interest in the reform of African politics carry run counter to those which the donors have tried to push. Quite apart from the instrumentalist approach which the donors adopt to the democracy question in Africa, their overwhelmingly managerial and technicist operationalisation of the issue of governance does not strike a chord with the explicitly political perspectives developed by the forces in the vanguard of the campaign for the democratisation of Africa. Many of the activists emphasise, in their articulation of the African democratic project, political as well as economic and social elements. Democracy for them is not just a question of multi-party politics and electioneering even if the right of the people to freely elect their leaders is recognised as non-negotiable; it includes a vast array of social and economic reforms whose adoption is widely perceived as being necessary for the establishment of a more just social order. It is a definition of democracy which necessarily calls for an interventionist, "developmentalist" state, not for the unbridled retrenchment of the state. It calls for the thorough reforming of the state and its broad-ranging restructuring in order to tackle the problem of state failure but it also firmly rejects the World Bank/IMF programme for the redefinition of the role of the state. For these groups, there is a fundamental incompatibility between structural adjustment and democratisation and this is brought out by the experiences at the various national conferences in parts of Francophone Africa.

From Benin Republic to the Congo, Niger and Mali to Chad, and even the Democratic Republic of Congo (formerly Zaire), the main issues which dominated the agenda of the national conferences not only relate to administrative and political reforms, the limiting of the powers of the executive, the subordination of the military to the authority of elected politicians, the strengthening of the judiciary and its independence, and the re-organisation of the military under civilian governmental authority but also to far-reaching economic reforms based on a "developmentalist" state. Stinging criticisms against IMF/World Bank structural adjustment programmes have been commonplace even as many of the conferences acknowledge the necessity for far-reaching economic reforms in order to stem the tide of African economic decline (see Box 7). There was a recognition too of the need

Box 7: The Sovereign National Conference of Niger and the management of the country's economic crisis

Niger's Sovereign National Conference was declared open on 29 July, 1991. It sat for four months and attracted the participation of 1,200 delegates representing trade unions, students' unions, 30 political parties, voluntary associations, the civil service, religious groups, the chamber of commerce, etc. Its proceedings were broadcast live on the national radio so that all residents of the country could follow the debates.

One of the issues which attracted some of the most intense debate and passion was the economic and financial crisis facing the country. This was not surprising as the state was virtually bankrupt before the conference was convened. For many of the delegates, there was no doubt that such a dire situation required bold measures. They were however less sure that the adjustment policies of the IMF and the World Bank that had been implemented for several years provided the appropriate framework for remedial action and the reasons which they gave were legion, not least among them the huge social costs exacted by the programme. However, the conference decided to listen to the arguments of officials of the IMF and the World Bank, who had been attending the Conference as observers, as to why Niger should stick to their orthodox programme rather than search for an alternative.

Most of the conferences were, however, unimpressed by the views presented by the Bank and Fund officials and they voted to reject their structural adjustment programme. The government was mandated to develop an alternative programme on the basis of which Niger might be ushered out of its prolonged crisis.

Source: Ibrahim (1996), p. 58

to strengthen state capacity even as the democratisation of state structures and procedures is undertaken. Quite clearly, popular perception within Africa on the reform of African economies and the democratisation of the state and society run counter to the views held and pushed by the donors, especially the World Bank.

Turning to the question of capacity-building which has featured in the discussion on governance and structural adjustment, and in support of which the World Bank launched an African Capacity Building Foundation, it has been argued and demonstrated by critics that donor-driven market reforms have contributed substantially to undermining indigenous capacity in Africa. While few will doubt that the availability in abundance of professionally competent economists, policy analysts, managers, auditors, jurists and other professionals is essential to the promotion of "good" governance, the experience of the last decade under the regime of structural adjustment and its associated authoritarianism has, as we noted earlier, been an exacerbation of the brain drain from Africa. Hordes of highly qualified personnel, trained at great expense to their countries, unable to cope with or accept the social, economic, and political costs of adjustment, have sought greener pastures in Europe, North America, and the Middle East. For some, frustration, arising out of the lack of basic equipment with which to perform their tasks and an anxiety to keep abreast of changes in their professional fields have been the factors motivating the decision to leave their countries. Those professionals who, for whatever reason, have stayed behind have either had to engage in moonlighting in order to earn extra money to supplement their diminishing real income or have opted for political appointments which are often unrelated to their professional training.

Without diminishing the importance of human resource development to the transformation of Africa, the politics of the World Bank's capacity building initiative for the continent ought to be exposed for what it is, namely that it is an initiative aimed at generating a ready intellectual and professional constituency for the Bank's adjustment programmes. In this regard, it would be correct to argue that the initiative continues the World Bank's recent practice of defining the competence of the African professional in terms of the professional's willingness to imbibe and follow the institution's current approach to macro-economic and other policy changes in Africa. Many an African professional who has refused to see the world through the Bank's lenses has been dismissed as lacking in skill or denigrated as "rent seekers".

Given that a majority of African intellectuals are either hostile to or sceptical about the Bank's neo-liberal economic reform project in the countries of the continent, it is little wonder that the institution has strongly sought to push an exaggerated version of the view that Africa lacks a competent professional class. Clearly then, the Bank's capacity-building programme is an attempt to produce professionals who will support structural adjustment and extend its logic to their spheres of competence. This way, it should be possible to claim that adjustment measures are home-grown or that the adjusting governments are really the owners of the programmes. The issue of capacity building for strengthening democracy is not one that concerns the Bank. Indeed, in the need for Africa's technocratic/professional class to be insulated from society, the Bank seeks to diminish accountability to the people by their governors. An insulated technocracy, unresponsive to democratic pressures and accounting only to donors is bound to be a recipe for continued authoritarianism.

The disorientation and paralysis which many an African civil service has suffered have also been the fate of the educational sector where, in the face of Bank-inspired reforms, academics, students, and university administrative staff have felt compelled to embark on struggles to protect their rights and interests. These struggles have covered a broad range of issues, including pay, the content of the curriculum, the courses that are taught, the attempts at importing and imposing expatriate "experts" receiving internationally competitive salaries paid in foreign exchange on the universities even as their local colleagues continue to suffer collapses in their real income, the imposition of cost recovery measures, and the continuing decay of facilities and infrastructure, including libraries. The authoritarian responses of the state to these struggles and the unwillingness of the Bank, for a variety of reasons, to yield ground has meant that many African institutions of higher learning have been crippled by a cycle of protest strikes with costly consequences for the economies of various countries. It is ironic that in an era when the Bank claimed to have integrated governance into its repertoire of policies, academic freedom and access to education have never seemed more threatened in the African post-colonial experience.[7]

Beyond Structural Adjustment and towards Democratic Governance in Africa

Fifteen years after structural adjustment made its grand entry into the African economic crisis management environment, debates have continued regarding its efficacy both as a macro-economic model and as a framework for tackling the continent's crisis of governance. As part of these debates, attempts have been made to argue the case for tempering the social costs of adjustment and prescribe alternatives to the neoliberal project. Perhaps the best known of these is UNICEF's plea, made in 1987, for adjustment with a human face and the Economic Commission for Africa (ECA)'s blueprint entitled *African Alternative Framework to Structural Adjustment Programme for Socio-Economic Recovery and Transformation (AFF-SAP)* published in 1991. But both the UNICEF and ECA critique of the adjustment experience in Africa have been overwhelmingly concerned with the macro-economic and macro-social aspects of structural adjustment and although they inevitably enter into a discussion of the market-state dynamic, governance questions remain underdeveloped in their discourses.

Thus, although it is clear that the donor approach to governance which we have focused on in this study leaves a lot to be desired, the task of fashioning out an alternative remains to be undertaken. We offer here broad principles that could inform such an endeavour. In doing so, our concern is for a system of *democratic governance* in Africa within which the search for economic recovery can be undertaken. In our view, there can be no trade off between democratic governance and economic recovery/growth in Africa; both are necessary and desirable and should be seen as going together beyond the managerial populism that serves as the framework for the donor endeavour.

The starting point in the quest for an alternative framework for governance which, by definition and in practice, is democratic is the need to recognise from the outset that the project must not be subordinated to the goals and exigencies of structural adjustment or, for that matter, any other economic model discussion of which is foreclosed because it is seen as something inherently right or inevitable or both. The tragedy of the donor approach to governance is that, *ab initio*, it was constructed with a view to facilitating/accommodating an essentially unreconstructed economic reform model that was itself already the object of much contestation.

Within the framework of the donor approach, the question that was posed was: How can the governance programme be employed to facilitate the implementation of "painful" but "necessary" economic reforms? As Mkandawire (1996) has noted, this way of posing the governance question is premised on a certain perverse approach to politics which has dominated the literature in recent times. Under this approach, "politics is reduced to servicing a technocratically defined "welfare function" instead of technocrats devising the instruments necessary to meet a *democratically specified* "social welfare function" (Mkandawire, 1996:40). This, inevitably, limits the scope for democratic governance by foreclosing debates on a possible economic reform model. It undermines the political capacity of the state to strike the compromises and consensus necessary for policy implementation generally. It also prevents discussions that are necessary within the local policy bureaucracy. For Mkandawire, as for us and many others, the central question to be posed is: How do you carry out economic reform projects without undermining democratic governance and its consolidation? (Mkandawire, 1996; Olukoshi, 1996; Beckman, 1992; Amadeo and Banuri, 1991).

In view of the extremely limited results that have flowed from structural adjustment implementation and the huge costs which the programme has exacted, it is clear that the quest for an alternative framework for democratic governance will entail revisiting the question of the kind of policy package that is required for reforming the economies of the continent and restoring them to the path of growth. In doing this, several points of principle will need to be taken cognisance of. At one level, it will be necessary to recognise that in Africa, there can be no question of a trade-off between the state and the market; the state does have a decisive role to play in the developmental process and its reinstatement, without the encumbrances which previously undermined its efficacy, must be a central concern of post-adjustment Africa (Mkandawire, 1995; Olukoshi, 1996).

At another level, the creation of a political and institutional framework through which democratic demands can be made on the developmental state is a task which must also be seen as central to this process. What this suggests is that policies generally and economic reform policies in particular ought to be underpinned by a clear social consensus if they are ultimately to play a part in reinforcing the legitimacy of the state and consolidating democratic governance. The establishment of a social consensus is the surest path to a sound foundation for domestic "ownership" of economic reform policy. Furthermore, the tendency to reify the market "... into a neutral, apolitical and ahistorical institution" or to fetishise it with "... human attributes such as 'anger', 'disappointment', 'displeasure', 'nervousness' ..." (Mkandawire, 1996:36) which has been a by-product of global neo-liberalism will have to be discarded in favour of strategies for making the market accountable to the state and the state to the people (UNRISD, 1995; Olukoshi, 1996).

The question of the centrality of domestic social consensus to the quest for economic reform and the prospects for democratic governance have been brought to the fore by the experiences of those African countries which, during the late 1980s and early 1990s, made a transition from military or single party rule to multi-party forms of politics. Without exception, the elected governments of those countries, several of which consist of a new coalition of forces, have had to stick to the donor economic adjustment project whether or not there is domestic popular support for the programme and without opening up an internal debate on the issue. On account of a number of factors, including unrefined donor conditionality, Africa's elected governments have been confronted with a choicelessness as far as economic policy is concerned, a bizarre state of affairs since democracy is, partly at least, supposed to be about choice. In sticking to the neo-liberal reform project, several of the elected governments have presided over the undermining/dissolution of the coalition of mostly anti-adjustment forces that propelled them to power in the first place. They have also found it difficult to submit the adjustment packages to full and open parliamentary scrutiny, preferring instead to muscle parliament or resort to executive fiat.

As their popular support base has shrunk, many of Africa's elected governments, those very same regimes whose inauguration was supposed to signal the dawn of a new day in Africa, have increasingly become more authoritarian—and corrupt—to a point where many have found it difficult to distinguish between them and the *ancien regime* which they replaced (Beckman, 1992; Olukoshi, 1995; Mkandawire, 1996). This recourse to authoritarianism, and the flowering of corrupt practices associated with it, has repeatedly threatened the parliamentary coalition of the government of Bakili Muluzi in Malawi, severely discredited the Chiluba regime in Zambia, permitted an opportunistic military *coup d'état* in Niger, paved the way for the defeat of the Soglo regime in Benin and the return of Matthew Kerekou to power, resulted in an increasing public exhibition of intolerance in Ghana by an increasingly intemperate Jerry Rawlings. It is because of this that several scholars have argued that the manner in which the orthodox adjustment packages the elected governments of Africa have been compelled to stick to are packaged and sealed "... pose(s) serious problems to the consolidation of democracy in Africa" because their "... rigid prerequisites, inflexible built-in positions and the proliferation of cross-conditionalities ... force decision-makers into a take-it-or-leave-it corner, ruling out dialogue or creative political compromises within society at large" (Mkandawire, 1996:34).

Africa's post-adjustment strategy for economic reform and democratic governance, must, if it is to overcome the failings and shortcomings of the pre- and post-political reform, orthodox adjustment years, aim at the adoption of economic policy measures which are the product of a domestic social contract and which strengthen, rather than weaken and/or undermine fragile democratic institutions and processes that are in need of consolidation. The necessity for the policy measures to be sensitive to the social/welfare aspirations of the populace cannot be overemphasised. Few doubt that drastic measures need to be undertaken to reform African economies and polities. However, such drastic reform efforts stand a better chance of being achieved where they are built into a negotiated social contract in whose making various interest groups have a stake. The contract will also provide a framework within which state and governmental legitimacy can be reconstructed for the formulation and implementation of policies. Groups are not inherently averse to making sacrifices, including taking cuts in their consumption levels, where they are satisfied that these are temporary measures carried out within the boundaries of a negotiated social bargain in which they are stake holders.[10]

The construction of a social contract at this time will require a concerted attack on policy making "traditions" and structures which are part and parcel of authoritarianism on the continent. At one level, this will involve efforts at dismantling the authoritarian logic that permeates the existing patterns of donor-recipient relations. At another level, it will entail the recovery by domestic policy and political forces of the initiative for reform design and implementation as sanctioned through democratic institutions and processes. Furthermore, it will entail closer attention to the impact of economic reform instruments and policies and a recognition of the limits of the state's political capacity as dictated by the balance of social forces. It is precisely the failure to come to terms with these factors or the attempt to "manage" them out of existence that has ensured that the quest for democratic governance in Africa has proved elusive. But it need not be so.

Endnotes

1. Although many Bank publications continue to be suffused with claims that the orthodox adjustment programmes are indeed working (see, for a recent example, World Bank, 1994b), the increasing realisation that the market reform policies have failed to deliver the "accelerated development" promised by the Berg Report (World Bank, 1981) and the "sustained growth" (World Bank, 1989) that was announced with a fanfare in 1989 has generally compelled the Bretton Woods institution to be more circumspect about its claims and this is attested by several critical internal documents to which this author and many others have had access. As Mkandawire (1996:30) has noted, "... although the foot soldiers in the field still battle on fervently and the bravado still shows up in the public relations documents", the World Bank has, in the face of clear evidence of the lacklustre performance of its adjustment policies, "... sobered up a little about its claims and the spartan certainty with which it pushed its programmes".

2. For a summary of some of the evidence on the limited achievements of structural adjustment, see Elbadawi *et al.*, 1992; Mosley and Weeks, 1993; Ajayi, 1994; Engberg-Pedersen, 1996; and Mkandawire, 1996, among many others. For a good critique of the theoretical assumptions of the adjustment model, see Tarp, 1993. Concern about the limited achievements of structural adjustment was aired as much by radical as by sympathetic critics of the Bank and the IMF.

3. According to Agarwala and Schwartz (World Bank, 1994b), the contributions of African social scientists who were consulted during the preparation of the Bank's 1989 long-term perspective report was also central to this "paradigmatic shift". As members of the African Advisory Group which the Bank had set up, these social scientists pointed to several issues which centred on the socio-political context of policy-making and implementation. Their insistence on these issues contributed to the embrace by the institution of issues of governance in its work. Even if this interpretation of the African "contribution" to the emergence of the governance question is accepted, and there are many who will dispute it and opt for a co-optationist interpretation, it is still a moot point whether the "influence" of the social scientists has had any impact on the day-to-day policy-making of the main multilateral financial institutions.

4. Taking a global-historical approach, Samuel Huntington (1991) celebrates Legum's Africa-specific "second liberation" as being part of the "third wave" of democratisation that encapsulates the political reforms that were undertaken in Iberia in the mid-1970s, followed shortly after by those that swept through Latin America and Asia, culminating in the wave of reforms that shook the countries of the Soviet bloc during the late 1980s.

5. This perspective is, of course, derived from the long-standing position that liberal democracy and "free" markets go together. It has recently been restated in a most crude manner, replete with post-Cold War ideological and political triumphalism, by Fukuyama (1992) in his celebration of an end-state of history towards which the world has, teleologically, been moved.

6. In support of this position, the World Bank has recently been investing a considerable amount of resources, including staff time, to studying ways in which the "... structural and functional disconnect between informal, indigenous institutions rooted in the (Africa) region's history and culture and formal institutions mostly transplanted from outside" (Dia, 1996: 1) can be bridged.

7. The education sector reforms which the Bank attempted to undertake in African universities attracted some of the most concerted resistance to the entire adjustment package as students and faculty contested what they saw as efforts to commercialise education and undermine university autonomy and academic freedom. All over Africa, the expansion of access to education was considered one of the most important goals of post-colonial governance. It was a central element of the post-colonial "social contract". Among many students, education is seen as a right and not a privilege; there are many other groups that will agree with them. The attempts to subject the educational sector to a market logic therefore touched on a raw nerve; resistance by students and faculty resulted in further paralysis in the educational sector. A CODESRIA-supported conference which was held in Kampala, Uganda, discussed the crisis of the educational system in Africa and its highpoint was the adoption of a resolution on academic freedom in Africa.

8. There is an assumption in much of the work of the Bank that free debate and political liberalisation will, ineluctably, produce a political consensus in favour of orthodox adjustment policies. This instrumentalist approach is clearly spelt out in the Bank's 1994 report where it is stated, *inter alia*, that although "... the process of political transition may initially slow down the process of economic reform", greater political openness "... will lead to the opening of national dialogue and debate over reforms ... and contribute to a national sense of ownership of the reform process" and "... to the emergence of good governance" (World Bank, 1994b). The possibility that the process of political liberalisation might produce an outcome that results in the complete rejection or major modification of the economic reform package is, apparently, not one that is contemplated.

9. During the course of the 1980s and 1990s, World Bank resident representatives in African countries took on a higher profile and reserved the right to make open and behind-the-door comments about the economic policies of governments and any other subject, including the size and composition of the cabinet, that caught their fancy. Mkandawire (1996:38) has noted correctly that, backed by the threat of the application of conditionality in the context of a system of donor and creditor cartelisation over which the Bank presided, their pronouncements "... acquired Delphic proportions" which few governments could afford to ignore.

10. In Nigeria, following the onset in the early 1980s of a national economic crisis, negotiations were opened between the incumbent civilian government of Shehu Shagari and the IMF for a loan. This, however, met with widespread domestic opposition which compelled that regime and its successor, the military junta of General Muhammadu Buhari, to refuse to accept the central condition of the Fund for the national currency, the Naira, to be devalued. The Babangida junta which replaced the Buhari regime in 1985 committed itself to breaking the deadlock between the country and the IMF. This prompted nation-wide protests which forced the government to call for a national debate on the country's economic future. In the course of the debate, most Nigerians, individually, in groups, and through their associations, stated that they were emphatically opposed to the IMF and its loan conditionalities but that they were ready to make "sacrifices" for the sake of national economic recovery. Even men of the 82nd Airborne Division of the Army urged General Babangida, as their commander-in-chief, to resist Nigeria's enslavement by the Fund; they offered to take cuts in their salary as part of the sacrifice they were prepared to make. They, and many other Nigerians from all walks of life, took this position openly in spite of the fact that it was public knowledge that General Babangida and his economic advisers wanted a result that would endorse their willingness to embrace the IMF's reform package and the conditions associated with it (see Olukoshi, 1992).

References

Adamolekun, L. and C. Bryant (1994), *Governance Progress Report: The African Regional Experience*. Washington, DC: World Bank.

Ajayi, S. I. (1994), "State of the Macro-Economic Effectiveness of Structural Adjustment Programmes in Sub-Saharan Africa", in R. van der Hoeven and F. van der Kraaij (eds), *Structural Adjustment and beyond in Sub-Saharan Africa*. London: James Currey.

Amadeo, E. and T. Banuri (1991), "Policy Governance and Management of Conflict", in T. Banuri (ed), *Economic Liberalisation: No Panacea*. Oxford: Clarendon Press.

Anyang' Nyongo P. (ed) (1987), *Popular Struggles for Democracy in Africa*. London: Zed Books.

Azarya, V. and N. Chazan (1987), "Disengagement from the State in Africa: Reflections on the Experience of Ghana and Guinea", *Comparative Politics in Society and History*, Vol. 20, No. 1.

Bangura, Y. (1986), "Structural Adjustment and the Political Question", *Review of African Political Economy*, No. 37.

Bangura, Y. (1989a), "Crisis, Adjustment and Politics in Nigeria", *AKUT* 38, Uppsala.

Bangura, Y. (1989b), "Crisis and Adjustment: The Experience of Nigerian Workers", in B. Onimode (ed), *The IMF, the World Bank and the African Debt, Vol. 2, Social and Economic Impact*. London: Zed Books/IFAA.

Bangura, Y. and B. Beckman (1991), "African Workers and Structural Adjustment, with a Nigerian Case-Study", in D. Ghai (ed) (1991).

Bangura, Y. and P. Gibbon, (1992), "Adjustment, Authoritarianism and Democracy in Sub-Saharan Africa: An Introduction to Some Conceptual and Empirical Issues", in P. Gibbon, Y. Bangura and A. Ofstad (eds) (1992).

Bangura, Y. (1994a), "Economic Restructuring, Coping Strategies and Social Change: Implications for Institutional Development in Africa", *Development and Change*, Vol. 25, No. 4.

Bangura, Y. (1994b), *Intellectuals, Economic Reform and Social Change: Constraints and Opportunities in the Formation of a Nigerian Technocracy*, Dakar, CODESRIA Monograph Series.

Barkan, J. (1992), "The Rise and Fall of a Governance Realm in Kenya", in G. Hyden and M. Bratton (eds) (1992).

Bates, R. (1981), *Markets and States in Tropical Africa*. Berkeley: University of California Press.

Bates, R. and A. Krueger (eds) (1993), *Political and Economic Interactions in Economic Policy Reform: Evidence from Eight Countries*. Oxford: Blackwell.

Beckman, B. (1988a), "The Post-Colonial State: Crisis and Reconstruction", *IDS Bulletin*, Vol. 19, No. 4.

Beckman, B. (1988b), "Comments on Göran Hyden's State and Nation under Stress", in Swedish Foreign Ministry, *Recovery in Africa: A Challenge for Development Co-operation*. Stockholm: Foreign Ministry.

Beckman, B. (1989), "Whose Democracy? Bourgeois versus Popular Democracy in Africa", *Review of African Political Economy*, Nos. 45/46.

Beckman, B. (1990), "Structural Adjustment and Democracy: Interest Group Resistance to Structural Adjustment and the Development of the Democracy Movement in Africa". Stockholm, (Mimeo).

Beckman, B. (1992), "Empowerment or Repression?: The World Bank and the Politics of Adjustment", in P. Gibbon, Y. Bangura and A, Ofstad (eds) (1992).

Bratton, M. (1989), "Beyond the State: Civil Society and Associational Life in Africa", *World Politics*, Vol. XLI, No. 3.

Bratton, M. (1990), "Non-Governmental Organisations in Africa", *Development and Change*, Vol. 21, No. 1.

British High Commission, Lagos (1990), "Hurd Highlights Need for Good Government in Africa and Elsewhere", Press Release, 11 June.

Callaghy, T. (1989), "Towards State Capability and Embedded Liberalism in the Third World: Lessons for Adjustment", in J. Nelson (ed) 1990.

Callaghy, T. (1990), "Lost between State and Market: The Politics of Economic Adjustment in Ghana, Zambia and Nigeria", in J. Nelson (ed) (1990).

Campbell, B. (1989), "Structural Adjustment and Recession in Africa: Implications for Democratic Process and Participation". Atlanta, (Mimeo).

Carter Center (1989), *Perestroika Without Glasnost*. Atlanta: Africa Governance Programme of the Carter Center of Emory University.

Chazan, N. (1988), "Ghana: Problems of Governance and the Emergence of Civil Society", in L. Diamond, J. Linz and S. Lipset (eds) (1988).

Chaudry, K. (1993), "The Myths of the Markets and the Common History of Late Developers", *Politics and Society*, Vol. 21, No. 3.

Conable, B. (1991), "Reflections on Africa: The Priority of Sub-Saharan African Economic Development". Washington, DC: World Bank.

Cornia, G., R. Jolly and F. Stewart (eds) (1987), *Adjustment with a Human Face*. 2 Vols. Oxford: Clarendon Press.

Dia, M. (1993), *A Governance Approach to Civil Service Reform in Sub-Saharan Africa*. Washington, DC: World Bank Technical Papers No. 225.

Dia, M. (1996), *Africa's Management in the 1990s and beyond: Reconciling Indigenous and Transplanted Institutions*. Washington, DC: World Bank.

Diamond, L. (1988), "Roots of Failure, Seeds of Hope", in L. Diamond, J. Linz and S. Lipset (eds), *Democracy in Developing Countries. Vol. 2, Africa*. Boulder, CO: Lynne Reinner.

Diop, M. and M. Diouf (1990), *Le Senegal Sous Abdou Diouf*. Paris: Karthala.

ECA, (1989), *African Alternative Framework to Structural Adjustment Programmes for Socio-Economic Recovery and Transformation*. Addis Ababa: ECA.

Elbadawi, I., D. Ghura and G. Uwajaren (1992), *World Bank Adjustment Lending and Economic Performance in Sub-Saharan Africa*. Washington, DC: Policy Research Working Paper No. 1001.

Engberg-Pedersen, P. (1996), "The Politics of Good Development Aid: Behind the Clash of Aid Rationales", in K. Havnevik and B. van Arkadie (eds) (1996).

Engberg-Pedersen, P., P. Gibbon, P. Raikes and L. Udsholt (eds) (1996), *Limits to Adjustment in Africa: The Effects of Economic Liberalisation 1986–1994*. London: James Currey.

Fukuyama, F. (1992), *The End of History and the Last Man*. London: Penguin.

Ghai, D. (1991), *IMF and the South: Social Impact of Crisis and Adjustment*. London: Zed Books.

Gibbon, P., Y. Bangura and A. Ofstad (eds) (1992), *Authoritarianism, Democracy and Adjustment: The Politics of Economic Reform in Africa*. Uppsala: The Scandinavian Institute of African Studies.

Gibbon, P. (1992), "Structural Adjustment and Pressures toward Multipartyism in Sub-Saharan Africa", in P. Gibbon, Y. Bangura and A. Ofstad (eds) (1992).

Gibbon, P. and A. Olukoshi (1996), *Structural Adjustment and Socio-Economic Change in Sub-Saharan Africa: Some Conceptual, Methodological and Empirical Issues*. Uppsala: The Nordic Africa Institute.

Grindle, M. and J. Thomas (eds) 1991, *Public Choice and Policy Change: The Political Economy of Reform in Developing Countries*. Baltimore: Johns Hopkins University Press.

Haggard, S. and R. Kaufman (1989), "Economic Adjustment in New Democracies", in J. Nelson (ed) 1989.

Haggard, S. and R. Kaufman (eds) (1992), *The Politics of Economic Adjustment: International Constraints, Distributive Conflicts and the State*. Princeton, NJ: Princeton University Press.

Haggard, S. and S. Webb (eds) (1994), *Voting for Reform: Democracy, Political Liberalization and Economic Adjustment*. Oxford: Oxford University Press.

Havnevik, K. and B. van Arkadie (eds) (1996), *Domination or Dialogue: Experiences and Prospects for African Development Co-operation*. Uppsala: The Nordic Africa Institute.

Herbst, J. (1990), "The Structural Adjustment of Politics in Africa", *World Development*, Vol. 18, No. 7.

Huntington, S. P. (1991), *The Third Wave: Democratization in the Late Twentieth Century*. Norman: University of Oklahoma Press.

Hutchful, E. (1987), "The Crisis of the New International Division of Labour: Authoritarianism and the Transition to Free Market Economies in Africa", *Africa Development*, Vol. 12, No. 2.

Hyden, G. and M. Bratton (eds) (1992), *Governance and Politics in Africa*. Boulder, CO: Lynne Reinner.

Ibrahim, J. (1989), "The State, Accumulation, and Democratic Forces in Nigeria". Uppsala (Mimeo).

Ibrahim, J. (1990), "Expanding the Nigerian Democratic Space". Bordeaux, (Mimeo).

Ibrahim, J. (1996), "The Weakness of "Strong States": The Case of Niger Republic", in A. Olukoshi and L. Laakso (eds) (1996).

Joseph, R. (1989), "Governance in Africa", in Carter Center (1989).

Ka, S. and N. van de Walle (1994), "Senegal: Stalled Reform in a Dominant Party System", in S. Haggard and S. Webb (eds) (1994).

Killick, T. (1989), *A Reaction Too Far: Economic Theory and the Role of the State in Developing Countries*. London: Overseas Development Institute.

Lal, D. (1983), *The Poverty of Development Economics*. London: Institute of Economic Affairs, Hobarth Paperback 16.

Lal, D. (1987), "The Political Economy of Economic Liberalisation", *World Bank Economic Review*, Vol. 1, No. 2.

Landell-Mills, P. (1992), "Governance, Cultural Change and Empowerment", *Journal of Modern African Studies*, Vol. 30, No. 4.

Landell-Mills, P. and I. Serageldin (1991), "Governance and the External Factor", in *Proceedings of the World Bank Annual Conference on Development Economics*. Washington, DC: World Bank.

Legum, C. (1992), "The Postcommunist Third World: Focus on Africa", *Problems of Communism*, Vol. 41, Nos. 1–2.

Lindauer, D. and B. Nunberg (eds) (1996), *Rehabilitating Government: Pay and Employment Reform in Africa*. Washington, DC/Aldershort: World Bank and Avebury.

Mamdani, M., T. Mkandawire and E. Wamba-dia-Wamba (1988), *Social Movements , Social Transformations and the Struggle for Democracy in Africa*. Dakar: CODESRIA.

Mamdani, M. (1991), "Uganda: Contradictions in the IMF Programme and Perspective", in D. Ghai (ed) (1991).

Mamdani, M. and E. Wamba-dia-Wamba (eds) (1995), *African Studies in Social Movements and Democracy*. Dakar: CODESRIA Books.

Mkandawire, T. "Crisis and Adjustment in Sub-Saharan Africa", in D. Ghai (ed) (1991).

Mkandawire, T. (1992), "Adjustment with a Democratic Face", in G. Cornia, T. Mkandawire and R. van der Hoeven (eds), *Africa's Recovery in the 1990s: From Stagnation and Adjustment to Human Development*. London: Macmillan.

Mkandawire, T (1994), "Adjustment, Political Conditionality and Democratisation in Africa", in G. Cornia and G. Helleiner, *From Adjustment to Development in Africa: Conflict, Controversy, Convergence, Consensus?* London: Macmillan.

Mkandawire, T. (1995), "Beyond Crisis: Towards Democratic Developmental States in Africa". Dakar, (Mimeo).

Mkandawire, T. and A. Olukoshi (eds) (1995), *Between Liberalisation and Repression: The Politics of Structural Adjustment in Africa*. Dakar: CODESRIA Books.

Mkandawire, T. (1996), "Economic Policy-Making and the Consolidation of Democratic Institutions in Africa", in K. Havnevik and B. van Arkadie (eds) (1996).

Mosley, P. and J. Weeks (1993), "Has Recovery Begun? Africa's Adjustment in the 1980s Re-visited", *World Development*, Vol. 20, No. 10.

Mustapha, A. R. (1988), "Ever-Decreasing Circles: Democratic Rights in Nigeria, 1978–1988". Oxford, (Mimeo).

Mustapha, A. R. (1992), "Structural Adjustment and Multiple Modes of Livelihood in Nigeria", in P. Gibbon, Y. Bangura and A, Ofstad (eds) (1992).

Nelson, J. (ed) (1989), *Fragile Coalitions: The Politics of Economic Adjustment*. New Brunswick: Transaction Books.

Nelson, J. (ed) (1990), *Economic Crisis and Policy Choice: The Politics of Economic Adjustment in the Third World*. Princeton, NJ: Princeton University Press.

Nunberg, B. (1989), *Public Sector Pay and Employment Reform: A Review of the World Bank Experience*. Washington, DC: World Bank, Discussion Paper 68.

Nunberg, B. and J. Nellis (1990), "Civil Service Reform and the World Bank", PRE Working Paper 422. Washington, DC: World Bank.

Nyang'oro, J. and T. Shaw (eds) 1992, *Beyond Structural Adjustment in Africa: The Political Economy of Sustainable and Democratic Development*. New York: Praeger.

Olukoshi, A. (1991), "The Politics of Structural Adjustment in Nigeria". Uppsala, (Mimeo).

Olukoshi, A. (ed) (1992), *The Politics of Structural Adjustment in Nigeria*. London: James Currey.

Olukoshi, A. and L. Wohlgemuth (eds) (1995), *A Road to Development: Africa in the 21st Century*. Uppsala: The Nordic Africa Institute.

Olukoshi, A. (1995), "Africa: Democratising under Conditions of Economic Stagnation". Dakar (Mimeo).

Olukoshi, A. (1996), "The Impact of Recent Economic Reform Efforts on the State in Africa", in K. Havnevik and B. van Arkadie (eds) (1996).

Olukoshi, A. and L. Laakso (eds) (1996), *Challenges to the Nation-State in Africa*. Uppsala: The Nordic Africa Institute.

Robinson, D. (1990), *Civil Service Pay in Africa*. Geneva: ILO.

Rothchild, D. and N. Chazan (eds) (1988), *The Precarious Balance: State and Society in Africa*. Boulder, CO: Lynne Reinner.

Sandbrook, R. (1985), *The Politics of Africa's Economic Stagnation*. Cambridge: Cambridge University Press.

Sandbrook, R. (1986), "The State and Economic Stagnation in Tropical Africa", *World Development*, Vol. 14, No. 3.

Sandbrook, R. (1991), "Economic Crisis, Structural Adjustment and the State in Africa", in D. Ghai (ed) (1991).

Stokke, O. (ed) (1995), *Aid and Political Conditionality*. London: EADI/Frank Cass.

Tarp, F. (1993), *Stabilisation and Structural Adjustment: Macroeconomic Frameworks for Analysing the Crisis in Sub-Saharan Africa*. London: RKP.

UNRISD (1995), *States of Disarray: The Social Effects of Globalisation*. Geneva: UNRISD.

Wai, D. (1991), "Governance, Economic Development and the Role of External Actors". Oxford, (Mimeo.

Wai, D. (1994), *Political Change and Economic Development in Africa*. Washington, DC: World Bank.

Waterbury, J. (1989), "The Political Management of Economic Adjustment and Reform", in J. Nelson (ed) (1989).

Widner, J. (ed) (1992), *Economic Change and Political Liberalisation in Sub-Saharan Africa*. Baltimore, NJ: Johns Hopkins University Press.

World Bank (1981), *Accelerated Development in Sub-Saharan Africa: An Agenda for Action*. Washington, DC: World Bank.

World Bank (1989), *Sub-Saharan Africa: From Crisis to Sustainable Growth*. Washington, DC: World Bank.

World Bank (1990), *The Long-Term Perspective Study of Sub-Saharan Africa: Background Papers. Vol. 3, Institutional and Sociopolitical Issues*. Washington, DC: World Bank.

World Bank (1991), *The African Capacity Building Initiative: Towards Improved Policy Analysis and Development Management in Sub-Saharan Africa*. Washington, DC: World Bank.

World Bank (1992), *Governance and Development*. Washington, DC: World Bank.

World Bank (1994a), *Governance: The World Bank's Experience*. Washington, DC: World Bank.

World Bank (1994b), *Adjustment in Africa: Reforms, Results and the Road Ahead*. New York: Oxford University Press.

Publications of the research programme " Political and Social Context of Structural Adjustment in Africa" published by the Nordic Africa Institute

Gibbon P., Bangura and A. Ofstad (eds.), 1992, *Authoritarianism, Democracy and Adjustment. The Politics of Economic Reform in Africa*. Seminar proceedings no. 26.

Gibbon, P. (ed.), 1993, *Social Change and Economic Reform in Africa*.

Chachage, C.S.L., M. Ericsson and P. Gibbon, 1993, *Mining and Structural Adjustment. Studies on Zimbabwe and Tanzania*. Research report no. 92.

Neocosmos, M., 1993, *The Agrarian Question in Africa and the Concept of "Accumulation from Below". Economics and Politics in the Struggle for Democracy*. Research report no. 93.

Kanyinga. K., A.S.Z. Kiondo and P. Tidemand, 1994, *The New Local Level Politics in East Africa. Studies on Uganda, Tanzania and Kenya*. Edited and introduced by Peter Gibbon. Research report no. 95.

Osaghae, E.E., 1995, *Structural Adjustment and Ethnicity in Nigeria*. Research report no. 98.

Gibbon, P. (ed.), 1995, *Markets, Civil Society and Democracy in Kenya*.

Gibbon P. (ed.), 1995, *Structural Adjustment and the Working Poor in Zimbabwe*.

Gibbon, P., 1995, *Liberalised Development in Tanzania*.

Bijlmakers. L.A., M.T. Basset and D.M. Sanders, 1996, *Health and Structural Adjustment in Rural and Urban Zimbabwe*. Research report no. 101.

Gibbon, P. and A.O. Olukoshi, 1996, *Structural Adjustment and Socio-Economic Change in Sub-Saharan Africa. Some Conceptual, Methodological and Research Issues*. Research report no. 102.

Olukoshi. A.O. and L. Laakso (eds.), 1996, *Challenges to the Nation-State in Africa*.

Olukoshi, A.O. (ed.), 1998, *The Politics of Opposition in Contemporary Africa*.

Egwu, S.G., 1998, *Structural Adjustment, Agrarian Change and Rural Ethnicity in Nigeria*. Research report no. 103.

Olukoshi, A.O., 1998, *The Elusive Prince of Denmark. Structural Adjustment and the Crisis of Governance in Africa*. Research report no. 104.

Research Reports published by the Institute

Some of the reports are out of print. Photocopies of these reports can be obtained at a cost of SEK 0:50/page.

1. Meyer-Heiselberg, Richard, *Notes from Liberated African Department in the Archives at Fourah Bay College, Freetown, Sierra Leone*. 61 pp. 1967 (OUT-OF-PRINT)

2. Not published

3. Carlsson, Gunnar, *Benthonic Fauna in African Watercourses with Special Reference to Black Fly Populations*. 13 pp. 1968 (OUT-OF-PRINT)

4. Eldblom, Lars, *Land Tenure—Social Organiza-tion and Structure*. 18 pp. 1969 (OUT-OF-PRINT)

5. Bjerén, *Gunilla, Makelle Elementary School Drop-Out. 1967*. 80 pp. 1969 (OUT-OF-PRINT)

6. Møberg, Jens Peter, *Report Concerning the Soil Profile Investigation and Collection of Soil Samples in the West Lake Region of Tanzania*. 44 pp. 1970 (OUT-OF-PRINT)

7. Selinus, Ruth, *The Traditional Foods of the Central Ethiopian Highlands*. 34 pp. 1971 (OUT-OF-PRINT)

8. Hägg, Ingemund, *Some State-Controlled Industrial Companies in Tanzania. A Case Study*. 18 pp. 1971 (OUT-OF-PRINT)

9. Bjerén, Gunilla, *Some Theoretical and Methodological Aspects of the Study of African Urbanization*. 38 pp. 1971 (OUT-OF-PRINT)

10. Linné, Olga, *An Evaluation of Kenya Science Teacher's College*. 67 pp. 1971. SEK 45,-

11. Nellis, John R., *Who Pays Tax in Kenya?* 22 pp. 1972. SEK 45,-

12. Bondestam, Lars, *Population Growth Control in Kenya*. 59 pp. 1972 (OUT OF PRINT)

13. Hall, Budd L., *Wakati Wa Furaha. An Evalua-tion of a Radio Study Group Campaign*. 47 pp. 1973. SEK 45,-

14. Ståhl, Michael, *Contradictions in Agricultural Development. A Study of Three Minimum Package Projects in Southern Ethiopia*. 65 pp. 1973 (OUT-OF-PRINT)

15. Linné, Olga, *An Evaluation of Kenya Science Teachers College. Phase II 1970–71*. 91 pp. 1973 (OUT-OF-PRINT)

16. Lodhi, Abdulaziz Y., *The Institution of Slavery in Zanzibar and Pemba*. 40 pp. 1973. ISBN 91-7106-066-9 (OUT-OF-PRINT)

17. Lundqvist, Jan, *The Economic Structure of Morogoro Town. Some Sectoral and Regional Characteristics of a Medium-Sized African Town*. 70 pp. 1973. ISBN 91-7106-068-5 (OUT-OF-PRINT)

18. Bondestam, Lars, *Some Notes on African Statistics. Collection, Reliability and Interpretation*. 59 pp. 1973. ISBN 91-7106-069-4 (OUT-OF-PRINT)

19. Jensen, Peter Føge, *Soviet Research on Africa. With Special Reference to International Relations*. 68 pp. 1973. ISBN 91-7106-070-7 (OUT-OF-PRINT)

20. Sjöström, Rolf & Margareta, *YDLC—A Literacy Campaign in Ethiopia. An Introductory Study and a Plan for Further Research*. 72 pp. 1973. ISBN 91-7106-071-5 (OUT-OF-PRINT)

21. Ndongko, Wilfred A., *Regional Economic Planning in Cameroon*. 21 pp. 1974. SEK 45,-. ISBN 91-7106-073-1

22. Pipping-van Hulten, Ida, *An Episode of Colo-nial History: The German Press in Tanzania 1901– 1914*. 47 pp. 1974. SEK 45,-. ISBN 91-7106-077-4

23. Magnusson, Åke, *Swedish Investments in South Africa*. 57 pp. 1974. SEK 45,-. ISBN 91-7106-078-2

24. Nellis, John R., *The Ethnic Composition of Leading Kenyan Government Positions*. 26 pp. 1974. SEK 45,-. ISBN 91-7106-079-0

25. Francke, Anita, *Kibaha Farmers' Training Centre. Impact Study 1965–1968*. 106 pp. 1974. SEK 45,-. ISBN 91-7106-081-2

26. Aasland, Tertit, *On the Move-to-the-Left in Uganda 1969–1971*. 71 pp. 1974. SEK 45,-. ISBN 91-7106-083-9

27. Kirk-Greene, Anthony H.M., *The Genesis of the Nigerian Civil War and the Theory of Fear*. 32 pp. 1975. SEK 45,-. ISBN 91-7106-085-5

28. Okereke, Okoro, *Agrarian Development Pro-grammes of African Countries. A Reappraisal of Problems of Policy*. 20 pp. 1975. SEK 45,-. ISBN 91-7106-086-3

29. Kjekshus, Helge, *The Elected Elite. A Socio-Economic Profile of Candidates in Tanzania's Parliamentary Election, 1970*. 40 pp. 1975. SEK 45,-. ISBN 91-7106-087-1

30. Frantz, Charles, *Pastoral Societies, Stratifica-tion and National Integration in Africa*. 34 pp. 1975. ISBN 91-7106-088-X (OUT OF PRINT)

31. Esh, Tina & Illith Rosenblum, *Tourism in Developing Countries—Trick or Treat? A Report from the Gambia*. 80 pp. 1975. ISBN 91-7106-094-4 (OUT-OF-PRINT)

32. Clayton, Anthony, *The 1948 Zanzibar General Strike*. 66 pp. 1976. ISBN 91-7106-094-4 (OUT OF PRINT)

33. Pipping, Knut, *Land Holding in the Usangu Plain. A Survey of Two Villages in the Southern Highlands of Tanzania.* 122 pp. 1976. ISBN 91-7106-097-9 (OUT OF PRINT)

34. Lundström, Karl Johan, *North-Eastern Ethiopia: Society in Famine. A Study of Three Social Institutions in a Period of Severe Strain.* 80 pp. 1976. ISBN 91-7106-098-7 (OUT-OF-PRINT)

35. Magnusson, Åke, *The Voice of South Africa.* 55 pp. 1976. ISBN 91-7106-106-1 (OUT OF PRINT)

36. Ghai, Yash P., *Reflection on Law and Economic Integration in East Africa.* 41 pp. 1976. ISBN 91-7106-105-3 (OUT-OF-PRINT)

37. Carlsson, Jerker, *Transnational Companies in Liberia. The Role of Transnational Companies in the Economic Development of Liberia.* 51 pp. 1977. SEK 45,-. ISBN 91-7106-107-X

38. Green, Reginald H., *Toward Socialism and Self Reliance. Tanzania's Striving for Sustained Transition Projected.* 57 pp. 1977. ISBN 91-7106-108-8 (OUT-OF-PRINT)

39. Sjöström, Rolf & Margareta, *Literacy Schools in a Rural Society. A Study of Yemissrach Dimts Literacy Campaign in Ethiopia.* 130 pp. 1977. ISBN 91-7106-109-6 (OUT-OF-PRINT)

40. Ståhl, Michael, *New Seeds in Old Soil. A Study of the Land Reform Process in Western Wollega, Ethiopia 1975–76.* 90 pp. 1977. SEK 45,-. ISBN 91-7106-112-6

41. Holmberg, Johan, *Grain Marketing and Land Reform in Ethiopia. An Analysis of the Marketing and Pricing of Food Grains in 1976 after the Land Reform.* 34 pp. 1977. ISBN 91-7106-113-4 (OUT-OF-PRINT)

42. Egerö, Bertil, *Mozambique and Angola: Reconstruction in the Social Sciences.* 78 pp. 1977. ISBN 91-7106-118-5 (OUT OF PRINT)

43. Hansen, Holger Bernt, *Ethnicity and Military Rule in Uganda.* 136 pp. 1977. ISBN 91-7106-118-5 (OUT-OF-PRINT)

44. Bhagavan, M.R., *Zambia: Impact of Industrial Strategy on Regional Imbalance and Social Inequality.* 76 pp. 1978. ISBN 91-7106-119-3 (OUT OF PRINT)

45. Aaby, Peter, *The State of Guinea-Bissau. African Socialism or Socialism in Africa?* 35 pp. 1978. ISBN 91-7106-133-9 (OUT-OF-PRINT)

46. Abdel-Rahim, Muddathir, *Changing Patterns of Civilian-Military Relations in the Sudan.* 32 pp. 1978. ISBN 91-7106-137-1 (OUT-OF-PRINT)

47. Jönsson, Lars, *La Révolution Agraire en Algérie. Historique, contenu et problèmes.* 84 pp. 1978. ISBN 91-7106-145-2 (OUT-OF-PRINT)

48. Bhagavan, M.R., *A Critique of "Appropriate" Technology for Underdeveloped Countries.* 56 pp. 1979. SEK 45,-. ISBN 91-7106-150-9

49. Bhagavan, M.R., *Inter-Relations Between Technological Choices and Industrial Strategies in Third World Countries.* 79 pp. 1979. SEK 45,-. ISBN 91-7106-151-7

50. Torp, Jens Erik, *Industrial Planning and Development in Mozambique. Some Preliminary Considerations.* 59 pp. 1979. ISBN 91-7106-153-3 (OUT-OF-PRINT)

51. Brandström, Per, Jan Hultin & Jan Lindström, *Aspects of Agro-Pastoralism in East Africa.* 60 pp. 1979. ISBN 91-7106-155-X (OUT OF PRINT)

52. Egerö, Bertil, *Colonization and Migration. A Summary of Border-Crossing Movements in Tanzania before 1967.* 45 pp. 1979. SEK 45,-. ISBN 91-7106-159-2

53. Simson, Howard, *Zimbabwe—A Country Study.* 138 pp. 1979. ISBN 91-7106-160-6 (OUT-OF-PRINT)

54. Beshir, Mohamed Omer, *Diversity Regionalism and National Unity.* 50 pp. 1979. ISBN 91-7106-166-5 (OUT-OF-PRINT)

55. Eriksen, Tore Linné, *Modern African History: Some Historiographical Observations.* 27 pp. 1979. ISBN 91-7106-167-3 (OUT OF PRINT)

56. Melander, Göran, *Refugees in Somalia.* 48 pp. 1980. SEK 45,-. ISBN 91-7106-169-X

57. Bhagavan, M.R., *Angola: Prospects for Socialist Industrialisation.* 48 pp. 1980. ISBN 91-7106-175-4 (OUT OF PRINT)

58. Green, Reginald H., *From Südwestafrika to Namibia. The Political Economy of Transition.* 45 pp. 1981. SEK 45,-. ISBN 91-7106-188-6

59. Isaksen, Jan, *Macro-Economic Management and Bureaucracy: The Case of Botswana.* 53 pp. 1981, SEK 45,-. ISBN 91-7106-192-4

60. Odén, Bertil, *The Macroeconomic Position of Botswana.* 84 pp. 1981. SEK 45,-. ISBN 91-7106-193-2

61. Westerlund, David, *From Socialism to Islam? Notes on Islam as a Political Factor in Contemporary Africa.* 62 pp. 1982. SEK 45,-. ISBN 91-7106-203-3

62. Tostensen, Arne, *Dependence and Collective Self-Reliance in Southern Africa. The Case of the Southern African Development Coordination Conference (SADCC).* 170 pp. 1982. ISBN 91-7106-207-6 (OUT-OF-PRINT)

63. Rudebeck, Lars, *Problèmes de pouvoir populaire et de développement. Transition difficile en Guinée-Bissau.* 73 pp. 1982. ISBN 91-7106-208-4 (OUT-OF-PRINT)

64. Nobel, Peter, *Refugee Law in the Sudan. With The Refugee Conventions and The Regulation of Asylum Act of 1974.* 56 pp. 1982. SEK 45,-. ISBN 91-7106-209-2

65. Sano, Hans-Otto, *The Political Economy of Food in Nigeria 1960–1982. A Discussion on Peasants, State, and World Economy.* 108 pp. 1983. ISBN 91-7106-210-6 (OUT-OF-PRINT)

66. Kjærby, Finn, *Problems and Contradictions in the Development of Ox-Cultivation in Tanzania.* 164 pp. 1983. SEK 60,-. ISBN 91-7106-211-4

67. Kibreab, Gaim, *Reflections on the African Refugee Problem: A Critical Analysis of Some Basic Assumptions.* 154 pp. 1983. ISBN 91-7106-212-2 (OUT-OF-PRINT) (

68. Haarløv, Jens, *Labour Regulation and Black Workers' Struggles in South Africa.* 80 pp. 1983. SEK 20,-. ISBN 91-7106-213-0

69. Matshazi, Meshack Jongilanga & Christina Tillfors, *A Survey of Workers' Education Activities in Zimbabwe, 1980–1981.* 85 pp. 1983. SEK 45,-. ISBN 91-7106-217-3

70. Hedlund, Hans & Mats Lundahl, *Migration and Social Change in Rural Zambia.* 107 pp. 1983. SEK 50,-. ISBN 91-7106-220-3

71. Gasarasi, Charles P., *The Tripartite Approach to the Resettlement and Integration of Rural Refugees in Tanzania.* 76 pp. 1984. SEK 45,-. ISBN 91-7106-222-X

72. Kameir, El-Wathig & I. Kursany, *Corruption as a "Fifth" Factor of Production in the Sudan.* 33 pp. 1985. SEK 45,-. ISBN 91-7106-223-8

73. Davies, Robert, *South African Strategy Towards Mozambique in the Post-Nkomati Period. A Critical Analysis of Effects and Implications.* 71 pp. 1985. SEK 45,-. ISBN 91-7106-238-6

74. Bhagavan, M.R. *The Energy Sector in SADCC Countries. Policies, Priorities and Options in the Context of the African Crisis.* 41 pp. 1985. SEK 45,-. ISBN 91-7106-240-8

75. Bhagavan, M.R. *Angola's Political Economy 1975–1985.* 89 pp. 1986. SEK 45,-. ISBN 91-7106-248-3

76. Östberg, Wilhelm, *The Kondoa Transformation. Coming to Ggrips with Soil Erosion in Central Tanzania.* 99 pp. 1986. ISBN 91-7106-251-3 (OUT OF PRINT)

77. Fadahunsi, Akin, *The Development Process and Technology. A Case for a Resources Based Development Strategy in Nigeria.* 41 pp. 1986. SEK 45,-. ISBN 91-7106-265-3

78. Suliman, Hassan Sayed, *The Nationalist Movements in the Maghrib. A Comparative Approach.* 87 pp. 1987. SEK 45,-. ISBN 91-7106-266-1

79. Saasa, Oliver S., *Zambia's Policies towards Foreign Investment. The Case of the Mining and Non-Mining Sectors.* 65 pp. 1987. SEK 45,-. ISBN 91-7106-271-8

80. Andræ, Gunilla & Björn Beckman, *Industry Goes Farming. The Nigerian Raw Material Crisis and the Case of Textiles and Cotton.* 68 pp. 1987. SEK 50,-. ISBN 91-7106-273-4

81. Lopes, Carlos & Lars Rudebeck, *The Socialist Ideal in Africa. A Debate.* 27 pp. 1988. SEK 45,-. ISBN 91-7106-280-7

82. Hermele, Kenneth, *Land Struggles and Social Differentiation in Southern Mozambique. A Case Study of Chokwe, Limpopo 1950–1987.* 64 pp. 1988. SEK 50,- ISBN 91-7106-282-3

83. Smith, Charles David, *Did Colonialism Capture the Peasantry? A Case Study of the Kagera District, Tanzania.* 34 pp. 1989. SEK 45,-. ISBN 91-7106-289-0

84. Hedlund, Stefan & Mats Lundahl, *Ideology as a Determinant of Economic Systems: Nyerere and Ujamaa in Tanzania.* 54 pp. 1989. SEK 50,-. ISBN 91-7106-291-2

85. Lindskog, Per & Jan Lundqvist, *Why Poor Children Stay Sick. The Human Ecology of Child Health and Welfare in Rural Malawi.* 111 pp. 1989. SEK 60,-. ISBN 91-7106-284-X

86. Holmén, Hans, *State, Cooperatives and Development in Africa.* 87 pp. 1990. SEK 60,-. ISBN 91-7106-300-5

87. Zetterqvist, Jenny, *Refugees in Botswana in the Light of International Law.* 83 pp. 1990. SEK 60,-. ISBN 91-7106-304-8

88. Rwelamira, Medard, *Refugees in a Chess Game: Reflections on Botswana, Lesotho and Swaziland Refugee Policies.* 63 pp. 1990. SEK 60,-. ISBN 91-7106-306-4

89. Gefu, Jerome O., *Pastoralist Perspectives in Nigeria. The Fulbe of Udubo Grazing Reserve.* 106 pp. 1992. SEK 60,-. ISBN 91-7106-324-2

90. Heino, Timo-Erki, *Politics on Paper. Finland's South Africa Policy 1945–1991.* 121 pp. 1992. SEK 60,-. ISBN 91-7106-326-9

91. Eriksson, Gun, *Peasant Response to Price Incentives in Tanzania. A Theoretical and Empirical Investigation.* 84 pp. 1993. SEK 60,- . ISBN 91-7106-334-X

92. Chachage, C.S.L., Magnus Ericsson & Peter Gibbon, *Mining and Structural Adjustment. Studies on Zimbabwe and Tanzania.* 107 pp. 1993. SEK 60,-. ISBN 91-7106-340-4

93. Neocosmos, Michael, *The Agrarian Question in Southern Africa and "Accumulation from Below". Economics and Politics in the Struggle for Democracy.* 79 pp. 1993. SEK 60,-. ISBN 91-7106-342-0

94. Vaa, Mariken, *Towards More Appropriate Technologies? Experiences from the Water and Sanitation Sector.* 91 pp. 1993. SEK 60,-. ISBN 91-7106-343-9

95. Kanyinga, Karuti, Andrew Kiondo & Per Tidemand, *The New Local Level Politics in East Africa. Studies on Uganda, Tanzania and Kenya.* 119 pp. 1994. SEK 60,-. ISBN 91-7106-348-X

96. Odén, Bertil, H. Melber, T. Sellström & C. Tapscott. *Namibia and External Resources. The Case of Swedish Development Assistance.* 122 pp. 1994. SEK 60,-. ISBN 91-7106-351-X

97. Moritz, Lena, *Trade and Industrial Policies in the New South Africa.* 61 pp. 1994. SEK 60,-. ISBN 91-7106-355-2

98. Osaghae, Eghosa E., *Structural Adjustment and Ethnicity in Nigeria.* 66 pp. 1995. SEK 60,-. ISBN 91-7106-373-0

99. Soiri, Iina, *The Radical Motherhood. Namibian Women's Independence Struggle.* 115 pp. 1996. SEK 60,-. ISBN 91-7106-380-3.

100. Rwebangira, Magdalena K., *The Legal Status of Women and Poverty in Tanzania.* 58 pp. 1996. SEK 60,-. ISBN 91-7106-391-9

101. Bijlmakers, Leon A., Mary T. Bassett & David M. Sanders, *Health and Structural Adjustment in Rural and Urban Zimbabwe.* 78 pp. 1996. SEK 60,-. ISBN 91-7106-393-5

102. Gibbon, Peter & Adebayo O. Olukoshi, *Structural Adjustment and Socio-Economic Change in Sub-Saharan Africa. Some Conceptual, Methodological and Research Issues.* 101 pp. 1996. SEK 80,-. ISBN 91-7106-397-8

103. Egwu, Samuel G., *Structural Adjustment, Agrarian Change and Rural Ethnicity in Nigeria.* 124 pp. 1998. SEK 80,-. ISBN 91-7106-426-5

104. Olukoshi, Adebayo O., *The Elusive Prince of Denmark. Structural Adjustment and the Crisis of Governance in Africa.* 59 pp. 1998. SEK 80,-. ISBN 91-7106-428-1